Kate Chopin's
THE
AWAKENING

CURRENTLY AVAILABLE

BLOOM'S MAJOR DRAMATISTS

Anton Chekhov

Henrik Ibsen

Arthur Miller

Eugene O'Neill

Shakespeare's Comedies

Shakespeare's Histories

Shakespeare's Romances

Shakespeare's Tragedies

George Bernard Shaw

Tennessee Williams

BLOOM'S MAJOR NOVELISTS

Jane Austen

The Brontës

Willa Cather

Charles Dickens

William Faulkner

F. Scott Fitzgerald

Nathaniel Hawthorne

Ernest Hemingway

Toni Morrison

John Steinbeck

Mark Twain

Alice Walker

BLOOM'S MAJOR SHORT STORY WRITERS

William Faulkner

F. Scott Fitzgerald

Ernest Hemingway

O. Henry

James Joyce

Herman Melville

Flannery O'Connor

Edgar Allan Poe

J. D. Salinger

John Steinbeck

Mark Twain

Eudora Welty

BLOOM'S MAJOR WORLD POETS

Geoffrey Chaucer

Emily Dickinson

John Donne

T. S. Eliot

Robert Frost

Langston Hughes

John Milton

Edgar Allan Poe

Shakespeare's Poems & Sonnets

Alfred, Lord Tennyson

Walt Whitman

William Wordsworth

BLOOM'S NOTES

The Adventures of Huckleberry Finn

Aeneid

The Age of Innocence

Animal Farm

The Autobiography of Malcolm X

The Awakening

Beloved

Beowulf

Billy Budd, Benito Cereno, & Bartleby the Scrivener

Brave New World

The Catcher in the Rye

Crime and Punishment

The Crucible

Death of a Salesman

A Farewell to Arms

Frankenstein

The Grapes of Wrath

Great Expectations

The Great Gatsby

Gulliver's Travels

Hamlet

Heart of Darkness & The Secret Sharer

Henry IV, Part One

I Know Why the Caged Bird Sings

Iliad

Inferno

Invisible Man

Jane Eyre

Julius Caesar

King Lear

Lord of the Flies

Macbeth

A Midsummer Night's Dream

Moby-Dick

Native Son

Nineteen Eighty-Four

Odyssey

Oedipus Plays

Of Mice and Men

The Old Man and the Sea

Othello

Paradise Lost

A Portrait of the Artist as a Young Man

The Portrait of a Lady

Pride and Prejudice

The Red Badge of Courage

Romeo and Juliet

The Scarlet Letter

Silas Marner

The Sound and the Fury

The Sun Also Rises

A Tale of Two Cities

Tess of the D'Urbervilles

Their Eyes Were Watching God

To Kill a Mockingbird

Uncle Tom's Cabin

Wuthering Heights

Kate Chopin's
THE
AWAKENING

A CONTEMPORARY
LITERARY VIEWS BOOK

Edited and with an Introduction by
HAROLD BLOOM

3 5 7 9 8 6 4 2

The hardback of this edition has been cataloged as follows:

Library of Congress Cataloging-in-Publication Data

Kate Chopin's The awakening / edited and with an introduction by Harold Bloom.
p. 88   cm. — (Bloom's notes)
Includes bibliographical references and index.
ISBN 0-7910-4512-9 (hbk.) — 0-7910-4919-1 (pbk.)
1. Chopin, Kate, 1851-1904.   Awakening.   2. Women and literature—Louisiana—New Orleans—History—19th century.
3. New Orleans (La.)—In literature.   I. Bloom. Harold.   II. Series.
PS1294.C63A6434   1998
813'.4—dc21
98-17600
CIP

Chelsea House Publishers
1974 Sproul Road, Suite 400
Broomall, PA 19008-0914

Contents

User's Guide

This volume is designed to present biographical, critical, and bibliographical information on the author and the work. Following Harold Bloom's editor's note and introduction are a detailed biography of the author, discussing major life events and important literary works. Then follows a thematic and structural analysis of the work, which traces significant themes, patterns, and motifs. An annotated list of characters supplies brief information on the chief characters in the work.

A selection of critical extracts, derived from previously published material by leading critics, then follows. The extracts consist of statements by the author, early reviews of the work, and later evaluations up to the present. These items are arranged chronologically by date of first publication. A bibliography of the author's writings (including a complete list of all books written, cowritten, edited, and translated), a list of additional books and articles on the author and the work, and an index of themes conclude the volume.

Harold Bloom is Sterling Professor of the Humanities at Yale University and Henry W. and Albert A. Berg Professor of English at the New York University Graduate School. He is the author of twenty books and the editor of more than thirty anthologies of literary criticism.

Professor Bloom's works include *Shelley's Mythmaking* (1959), *The Visionary Company* (1961), *Blake's Apocalypse* (1963), *Yeats* (1970), *A Map of Misreading* (1975), *Kabbalah and Criticism* (1975), and *Agon: Towards a Theory of Revisionism* (1982). *The Anxiety of Influence* (1973) sets forth Professor Bloom's provocative theory of the literary relationships between the great writers and their predecessors. His most recent books include *The American Religion* (1992), *The Western Canon* (1994), and *Omens of Millennium: The Gnosis of Angels, Dreams, and Resurrection* (1996).

Professor Bloom earned his Ph.D. from Yale University in 1955 and has served on the Yale faculty since then. He is a 1985 MacArthur Foundation Award recipient and served as the Charles Elkot Norton Professor of Poetry at Harvard University in 1987–88. He is currently the editor of other Chelsea House series in literary criticism, including MAJOR LITERARY CHARACTERS, MODERN CRITICAL VIEWS, and WOMEN WRITERS OF ENGLISH AND THEIR WORKS.

Editor's Note

My Introduction disputes feminist interpretations of *The Awakening*, arguing instead that Edna, in the mode of Walt Whitman, awakens only to sublime narcissistic self-gratification, properly fulfilled by her ocean suicide.

Percival Pollard, writing in 1909, rather nastily says that the book reveals "the growth of animalism in a woman," after which Kenneth Eble defends Chopin's novel as being "frankly . . . about sex."

In Stanley Kauffmann's view, *The Awakening* is "existentialist," while Cynthia Griffin Wolff sees Edna as a "schizoid personality," and Judith Fryer judges the heroine as one who is doomed to relive her childhood.

James H. Justus severely insists that Edna awakens to nothing at all, after which Linda Huf declares that society is the culprit, because it sees poor Edna only as a woman.

The myth of Psyche is invoked by Rosemary F. Franklin, while Bonnie St. Andrews blames marriage for Edna's fate, and Barbara C. Ewell usefully expounds some aspects of Creole culture in the book.

Edna's groping for a language adequate to female desire is described by Dale M. Bauer, after which Elizabeth Fox-Genovese refreshingly argues that *The Awakening* is a personal story rather than a social document.

Peggy Skaggs finds literary naturalism to be *The Awakening*'s mode, while Michael T. Gilmore sees the novel's imagery to be more akin to Impressionism, and Andrew Delbanco invokes Marxism as an explanatory concept.

For Mary E. Papke, Edna's awakening is to memories of childhood, after which larger memories, of the Darwinian kind, are summoned up by Bert Bender.

Eminent feminist Elaine Showalter studies Guy de Maupassant's influence, while Lynda S. Boren discusses Edna's relationship to Mademoiselle Reisz.

This volume concludes with Joyce Dyer, who examines the symbolism of the parrot at the start of *The Awakening*.

Introduction

HAROLD BLOOM

There are several intrinsic affinities between Walt Whitman's poetry and *The Awakening*, which I will explore here. However, there is an ironical extrinsic similarity that I mention first, doubtless at some risk of giving offense. Whitman's poetry is now much written about by academic critics who care only for the homoerotic Walt; the poetry, to them, is of interest only insofar as it represents the poet's undoubted desires. Similarly, Kate Chopin's *The Awakening* is now a favorite work of feminist critics, who find in it a forerunner of Liberation. I regard all this with amiable irony, since so much of Whitman's best poetry is quite overtly autoerotic while Edna Pontellier's awakening is to her own "shifting, treacherous, fickle deeps," not so much of her soul (as Chopin carefully adds) but of her body. If *The Awakening* is a breakthrough, it is as the subtle female version of the self-gratification slyly celebrated by Goethe (in *Faust, Part Two*) and openly sung by Walt Whitman.

Though *The Awakening* follows in the path of Flaubert's *Madame Bovary*, it shares little with that formidable precursor. Emma Bovary indeed awakens, belatedly and tragically, but the narcissistic Edna singly drifts from one mode of reverie to another, until she drowns herself in the sea, which for her as for Whitman represents night and the mother, death and the inmost self. Far from being a rebel, moved by sympathy with victims of societal oppression, Edna is even more isolated at the end than before. It is a very peculiar academic fashion that has transformed Edna into any kind of a feminist heroine. The protagonist of *The Awakening* is her own victim, unless one agrees with Kathleen Margaret Lane's assertion that: "Edna awakens to the horrible knowledge that she can never, because she is female, be her own person." Late 19th-century Creole society was not Afghanistan under the rule of the Taliban or Iran under the Ayatollah Khomeini. Chopin shows it as having something of a hothouse atmosphere, but that alas does seem the only possible context for Edna, who in fact loves no one—not her children, husband, friends, or lovers—and whose awakening is only to the ecstasies of self-gratification.

The influence of Whitman is pervasive throughout *The Awakening*, and suggests that Chopin was deeply immersed in *Leaves of Grass*, particularly in the *Sea-Drift* poems, and in the *Lilacs* elegy for Lincoln. Gouvernail, the benign bachelor who is one of the guests at Edna's birthday party, had appeared earlier in Chopin's short story, "A Respectable Woman," where he recites part of Section 21 of *Song of Myself*: "Night of south winds—night of the large few stars!/Still nodding night—." The entire passage could serve as an epigraph for *The Awakening*.

> Press close bare-bosom'd night—press close magnetic
>   nourishing night!
> Night of south winds—night of the few large stars!
> Still nodding night—mad naked summer night.

This is the model for the ecstatic rebirth of Edna's self, a narcissistic self-investment that awards Edna a new ego. Had Edna been able to see that her awakening was to a passion for herself, then her suicide perhaps could have been avoided. Chopin, a very uneven stylist, nevertheless was erotically subtler than most of her critics have been. Edna emulates Whitman by falling in love with her own body: "observing closely, as if it were something she saw for the first time, the fine, firm quality and texture of her flesh." This stems from Whitman's grand proclamation: "If I worship one thing more than another it shall be the spread of my own body, or any part of it." When Edna awakens to self, she hears the voice of the sea, and experiences its Whitmanesque embrace: "The touch of the sea is sensuous, enfolding the body in its soft, close embrace." When the naked Edna enters the mothering sea for a last time, we hear an echo of the undulating serpentine death that Whitman welcomes in *When Lilacs Last in the Dooryard Bloom'd*: "The foamy wavelets curled up to her white feet and coiled like serpents about her ankles." Is this indeed a chant of Women's Liberation, or a siren song of a Whitmanesque Love-Death?

Biography of
Kate Chopin

(1851–1904)

Kate Chopin was born Katherine O'Flaherty in St. Louis, Missouri, on February 8, 1851. Her father, Thomas O'Flaherty, was an Irish immigrant who became a prosperous merchant before his death in a railway accident in 1855. Her mother, Eliza Faris, was descended from French Creole aristocrats. She attended the St. Louis Academy of the Sacred Heart, where she read copiously, learned to play the piano, became fluent in French, and passionately supported the Confederacy during the Civil War. Chopin became more interested in literature and creative storytelling after the deaths of her father, great-grandmother, and half-brother during these years. She graduated from the academy in 1868 and became a belle in St. Louis high society. She soon became aware of feminist social issues and became rebellious, complaining of the parties a belle was expected to attend, and of the young men at dances whose "only talent" resided in their feet. She began to smoke cigarettes and wrote a feminist fable, "Emancipation." She read and admired the works of Jane Austen, the Brontë sisters, George Eliot, and George Sand.

In 1870 she married Oscar Chopin, a twenty-five-year-old cotton trader, New Orleans native, and Creole. They lived first in New Orleans and then, with the failure of Chopin's business in 1879, on a plantation at a place called "La Cote Joyeuse." During her marriage she was an exemplary wife; according to her daughter, she was the "Lady Bountiful of the neighborhood," an engaging personality. During her marriage Chopin explored New Orleans on foot and by streetcar, writing about what she saw, attending the theater and the opera, and spending her vacations engaged in reading at Grand Isle, on the Gulf of Mexico, where *The Awakening* is set. After Oscar Chopin died of swamp fever in 1893 she returned, with her six children, to St. Louis and began to write sketches of Louisiana life for publication. In 1899 her first published poem, "If It Might Be," appeared in the magazine *America*. During the 1890s Chopin wrote more than one hundred short stories and hosted a salon in her home at 3317 Morgan Street. Her articles, poems, and stories were published in *Atlantic Monthly*, *Criterion*, *Harper's Young People*, *Vogue*, and the *St. Louis Dispatch*. Her books include *At Fault* (1890), *Bayou Folk* (1894), and *A Night at Acadie* (1897). In 1899 Chopin published her final novella, *The Awakening*. The book caused a critical furor that ended her literary career. The public condemned her candid treatment of a young married woman's sexual and spiritual awakening.

Kate Chopin died from a cerebral hemorrhage suffered after spending the day at the World's Fair in St. Louis, Missouri, on August 22, 1904.

Thematic and
Structural Analysis

Kate Chopin's *The Awakening*, published in 1899, caused a critical furor that ended her literary career. Readers were shocked not only by this story about a young woman in rebellion against her husband and her love for a younger man, but also by its frank treatment of sexuality. Most of this short tale, or *novella*, is told from the point of view of Edna Pontellier, the young wife, with the narrator providing occasional clarification. The effect of this limited point of view is impressionistic; that is, it presents subjective impressions rather than objective reality. The most prominent *motif*, or recurrent thematic element, is of "awakening," an image that recurs throughout the novella, as we shall see.

In **chapter one** Léonce Pontellier is at the summer colony of Grand Isle to visit his wife and two children for the weekend. He departs for the evening to spend time gambling and socializing with other men of his class, leaving Edna in the company of young Robert Lebrun. The "utter nonsense" of the conversation between Lebrun and Mrs. Pontellier bores him. Mr. Pontellier is a study in both complacency and impatience: Edna returns from the beach with a sunburn and he is disturbed that this "valuable piece of personal property [had] suffered some damage." He views Edna as his property and is comfortable with that relationship.

The atmosphere is languorous on the porch where Robert Lebrun and Edna Pontellier sit and talk on this summer afternoon (**chapter two**). They are well-matched, both young and eager to talk about themselves, yet interested in each other's stories.

The "awakening" motif first occurs in **chapter three**, when Mr. Pontellier returns from dinner late in the evening awakening Edna to tell her "anecdotes and bits of news and gossip that he had gathered during the day." He is discouraged that his wife, "the sole object of his existence," is too tired to be interested. In "a monotonous, insistent way" he reproaches Edna for her "habitual neglect of the children," claiming that one of the sleeping boys has a fever. She refuses to respond to her husband's interrogation; he finishes his cigar and falls asleep immediately. But Edna is wide awake. The contrast between the "tacit and self-understood" kindness of her husband and the "indescribable oppression" of their marriage "fill[s] her whole being with a vague anguish."

Chapter four focuses upon Mr. Pontellier's vague dissatisfaction with his wife: "It was something which he felt rather than perceived, and he never voiced the feeling without subsequent regret and ample atonement," as we saw in **chapter three**. Edna is not a "mother-woman," like the others that summer at Grand Isle; those who "idolized their children, worshipped their husbands, and esteemed it a holy privilege to efface themselves as individuals and grow wings as ministering angels." The tone of this description is both the sarcastic observation of the narrator and the heartfelt sentiment of Mr. Pontellier. Madame Ratignolle is one such woman whom Léonce Pontellier deems "the embodiment of every womanly grace and charm." Frankness and familiarity, or "freedom of expression," are characteristic of the Creole conversation among the summer colony guests but alien to Edna's northern background. Vivid in her memory is the shock of hearing Madame Ratignolle relate the "harrowing story of one of her *accouchements*" (birthings) to a male guest. A narrative tension, or conflict, develops throughout the story between Edna's habitual reserve and the "freedom of expression" of the Creole culture into which she has married. This tension foreshadows and constructs the terms of her suicide.

Robert Lebrun's position in the summer colony society is clarified in **chapter five**. Each summer he attaches himself to an interesting woman guest—usually a married one; this summer he is the "devoted attendant" of Mrs. Pontellier. They share an "advanced stage of intimacy and camaraderie" sitting among the women on the porch this summer afternoon. With mock-seriousness Robert mournfully comments upon Madame Ratignolle's cold cruelty to one who had adored her the summer before. She recalls that he was "a troublesome cat," while he compares himself to "an adoring dog." More to the point, she claims that her husband might have become jealous. All laugh because, as both the narrator and Edna understand, "the Creole husband is never jealous; with him the gangrene passion . . . has become dwarfed by disuse." Edna sketches Madame Ratignolle who is "seated there like some sensuous Madonna, with the gleam of the fading day enriching her splendid color." As a likeness, her portrait of Madame Ratignolle is a failure, and Edna crumples it in her hands, an act significant in two ways: We know that her work is untutored and inept. The act also suggests that, although the likeness fails in one sense, in another the work may have succeeded as an impressionistic image. As yet, Edna has no knowledge by which to define either her art or herself.

Chapter six is a brief psychological sketch of Edna's moment of awakening to "her position in the universe as a human being, [recognizing] her relations as an individual to the world within and about her." She is twenty-eight years old and at "the beginning of things." The "voice of the sea" is seductive to her, seeming to speak to her soul; its touch like a "sensuous . . . close embrace." This is a disturbing and dangerous point for Edna, and her "contradictory impulses" mirror the contradictory outcomes possible from this place of beginning: She may gain wisdom, or she may perish.

Edna's relationship with Adèle Ratignolle is the subject of **chapter seven**. Edna, with her "sensuous susceptibility to beauty" is attracted by the physical charm and the personality of this Creole woman. In the heat of the afternoon they sit together on the beach, Edna fanning her companion and contemplatively watching the sea. Adèle asks what she is thinking and Edna makes an effort to respond to what is only a rhetorical question. Adèle protests that it is "really too hot to think, especially to think about thinking." Edna confides in Madame Ratignolle that the sea reminds her of herself as a young girl, "walking through the green meadow again; idly, aimlessly, unthinking and unguided." Like a "first breath of freedom" Edna feels "intoxicated" as she reveals a small portion of her feelings to Madame Ratignolle. Adèle seems sympathetic; she holds Edna's hand "firmly and warmly," and strokes it "fondly." The physical affection startles Edna, who is unaccustomed to displays of warmth. Her girlhood infatuations with young men had been distant, cerebral; her friendships with women have been earnest; her girlfriends as "self-contained" as she. On her desk is a framed picture of an actor, a tragedian, which she sometimes kisses passionately when alone.

Madame Ratignolle warns Robert about a danger she perceives in Edna (**chapter eight**): "She is not one of us; she is not like us. She might make the unfortunate blunder of taking you seriously." Chastened by this warning Robert assures Madame Ratignolle that there is "no earthly possibility" Edna Pontellier will ever take him seriously. Impressionistic authorial intrusions describe the atmosphere of the scene, as in the satirical description of Madame Lebrun at her sewing machine: "A little black girl sat on the floor, and with her hands worked the treadle of the machine. The Creole woman does not take any chances which may be avoided of imperiling her health."

A few weeks after Robert's conversation with Madame Ratignolle, the families gather for dinner and casual entertainment (**chapter nine**). The scene is hectic and the atmosphere domestic and indulgent: After the children are sent to bed, Robert asks Edna if she would like to hear Mademoiselle Reisz play the piano. The introduction of this character, a well-known concert pianist and a guest with whom Edna is apparently well-acquainted, emphasizes Edna's self-containment and the reader's always limited knowledge of her. Mademoiselle Reisz agrees to play for the guests only because she likes Edna. We know only that Edna is "very fond of music" and that she "sometimes liked to sit in the room of mornings when Madame Ratignolle played or practiced." How this has earned Mademoiselle Reisz's affection remains a mystery. Edna is deeply affected by Mademoiselle Reisz's artistry: Although it "was not the first time she had heard an artist at the piano [p]erhaps it was the first time she was ready, perhaps the first time her being was tempered to take an impress of the abiding truth." The meaning of this may seem as obscure to the reader as it is to Edna.

After the party the Pontelliers, the Ratignolles, and Robert Lebrun walk to the beach for a late-night swim (**chapter ten**).

Edna has been taking instruction in swimming all summer, without success. The water has terrified her, until now. This evening she swims, "like a little tottering, stumbling, clutching child, who of a sudden realizes its powers, and walks for the first time alone, boldly and with over-confidence." This evening, she wants to swim "far out, where no woman had swum before." The "space and solitude" of the Gulf seem to enchant her, offering a place in which she might lose herself. For a moment, she is terrified by a "quick vision of death" that seems to kill her "soul." Afterward, she walks back to the house, alone. Madame Lebrun later remarks to Mr. Pontellier that his wife seems "capricious." He agrees that she is, but only "sometimes, not often."

Robert overtakes Edna and she confides in him that this night has seemed "like a night in a dream," that "[t]here must be spirits abroad to-night." Robert whispers to her that there are indeed spirits abroad, that on this date, at this time, "a spirit that has haunted these shores for ages rises up from the Gulf. . . . [to] seek one mortal to hold him company . . . [and] to-night he found Mrs. Pontellier." Edna is wounded by his banter, but "he could not tell her that he had penetrated her mood and understood." They reach the house and Edna rests in a hammock. Robert sits on the stairs near her and smokes a cigarette. Neither speak, but both are moved by the "first-felt throbbings of desire."

In **chapter eleven** an incident occurs between Mr. and Mrs. Pontellier that mirrors and contrasts the scene of companion-able silence between Edna and Robert in the preceding chapter; the motif of awakening is juxtaposed with the power of unconsciousness, represented by the overwhelming need for sleep. Edna refuses to leave the hammock and come to bed, as her husband insists. She recognizes that "her will had blazed up, stubborn and resistant," but at the same time, she feels "like one who awakens gradually out of a dream, a delicious, grotesque, impossible dream, to feel again the realities pressing into her soul." Léonce draws up a rocker near to her and smokes a cigar. At last overcome by the need for sleep Edna enters the house, pausing to ask her husband if he will follow: "Just as soon as I have finished my cigar," he responds.

After a "troubled and feverish sleep" Edna wakes early, moved by vague impulses, "as if she had placed herself in alien hands for direction, and freed her soul of responsibility." Impressionistic images of the day heighten the effect of Edna's disturbing dreams: Lovers stroll to meet the boat to the *Chênière Caminada*, to attend mass; a "lady in black, with her Sunday prayer-book, velvet and gold-clasped, and her Sunday silver beads" follows them; Monsieur Farival, in a straw hat, follows the lady in black, and a "young barefooted Spanish girl, with a red kerchief and a basket, follows Monsieur Farival; the "little negro girl who worked Madame Lebrun's sewing-machine" sweeps the gallery; Edna sends the girl to awaken Robert, to tell him to meet her. She has never requested his presence before; she "had never seemed to want him before." Mariequita, the Spanish girl, jealously asks Robert if Mrs. Pontellier is his "sweetheart." She is unimpressed to learn that she is "a married lady, and has two children;" she knows of a man who ran away with another man's wife.

Edna finds the atmosphere of the church at *Chênière Caminada* oppressive (**chapter thirteen**). She leaves the mass and Robert follows her, provoking some gossip among those from the boat who remain. He takes her to rest at the cottage of Madame Antoine. Sensuous images convey a sense of beauty and strangeness: "the voice of the sea whispering through the reeds;" a "jagged fence made of sea-drift;" a "mild-faced Acadian" boy draws water for her, the water "cool to her heated face." She notices, for the first time, the "fine, firm quality and texture of her flesh." She sleeps and wakes refreshed and "very hungry;" she tears a piece of bread from a loaf "with her strong, white teeth" and downs a glass of wine; she goes "softly out of doors," plucks an orange from a tree, and tosses it at Robert, who did not know that she had awakened. The rest of the party have returned to Grand Isle hours before, but Robert reassures her that Léonce will not worry, since "he knows you are with me." As night comes Edna and Robert sit in the grass as Madame Antoine tells them stories. Symbols of the world they have left behind and harbingers of the choice Edna will make for herself, "shadows lengthened and crept out like stealthy, grotesque monsters across the grass."

On their return from *Chênière Caminada* (**chapter fourteen**), as Edna waits for her husband to return from the hotel, she thinks about a song she and Robert sang as they crossed the bay: "The voice, the notes, the whole refrain haun[t] her memory."

In **chapter fifteen** Edna is stunned to discover that Robert is leaving for Mexico. He insists, unconvincingly, that this has been his desire for many years. Edna concludes that she is suffering again from "the symptoms of infatuation which she had felt incipiently as a child . . . and later as a young woman." With Robert's departure, she is being "denied that which her impassioned, newly awakened being demanded." What "that" is seems as vague and as fantastic as Robert's fanciful stories.

With Robert gone and the summer at Grand Isle nearly over (**chapter sixteen**), Edna finds her "only real pleasurable moments" in swimming. In a heated conversation with a baffled Madame Ratignolle she attempts to define her newly awakened sense of self: "I would give up the unessential; I would give my money, I would give my life for my children; but I wouldn't give myself. I can't make it more clear; it's only something which I am beginning to comprehend, which is revealing itself to me." This declaration will also mark the paradox of her ultimate awakening, her suicide.

In **chapter sixteen**, Mademoiselle Reisz emerges as one image of the life possible for a single woman of artistic sensibility in 1899. She mirrors and distorts Edna's emerging vision of selfhood. Although she warms to Edna, she is a disagreeable and solitary figure. Her aversion to swimming symbolizes the difference from Edna in her temperament. She is also a malicious gossip who nonetheless satisfies Edna's need to talk about Robert, no matter the subject.

In the six years that the Pontelliers have been married Edna has "religiously followed" a social schedule centered in their "charming" and "conventional" home in New Orleans (**chapter seventeen**). Mr. Pontellier is "very fond of walking about his house examining its various appointments and details, to see that nothing was amiss. He greatly valued his possessions, chiefly because they were his." Edna is one of these possessions and Léonce is unhappy with her household management;

the dinner displeases him and, as has happened often before, he leaves for "the club." In the past, these familiar scenes caused her regret and a belated rebuke to the cook. This evening, however, Edna is enraged; she smashes a vase and throws her wedding ring to the floor, attempting to crush it under her heel. The alarmed maid enters and picks up the ring, which Edna slips back upon her finger without comment.

The morning brings no change in her mood (**chapter eighteen**). Edna no longer has any interest in her home, her children, or her surroundings; they are "all part and parcel of an alien world which had suddenly become antagonistic." Edna gathers her best sketches to bring to Madame Ratignolle, still her most intimate friend. The beautiful and efficient Madame Ratignolle looks at Edna's drawings and proclaims that her "talent is immense." Although Edna knows that her friend's opinion is "next to valueless," she wants her praise and encouragement. Edna had hoped to find comfort and reassurance amidst the "domestic harmony" of the Ratignolle household but is instead depressed after she leaves. Unlike Adèle, Edna feels consumed by "life's delirium."

By **chapter nineteen** Edna has abandoned both household management and emotional outbursts, "going and coming as it suited her fancy, and, so far as she was able, lending herself to any passing caprice." The reader's inclination to cheer her independence is tempered by the knowledge that a penalty will be exacted for this freedom. Léonce suspects that she might be "growing a little unbalanced mentally." Paradoxically, the less Edna seems to be "herself" in his eyes the more she is "becoming herself." Her mood alternates between happiness at simply being alive and depression, "when life appeared to her like a grotesque pandemonium and humanity like worms struggling blindly toward inevitable annihilation."

On one such day she is determined to visit Mademoiselle Reisz, to hear her play the piano (**chapter twenty**). Edna must see Madame Lebrun to find Mademoiselle Reisz's address. Madame Lebrun shares Robert's letters from Vera Cruz and Mexico City, but Edna is "despondent" that she can detect no message to herself in them. She departs with Mademoiselle Reisz's address; Madame Lebrun and Victor remark to each other how beautiful she looks. In some way, Victor observes, "she doesn't seem like the same woman."

Mademoiselle Reisz lives in a small apartment crowded by a "magnificent piano" and little else. The "strikingly homely" musician is delighted to see Edna (**chapter twenty-one**), laughing with "a contortion of the face and all the muscles of the body." Edna is amazed when Mademoiselle Reisz reveals that she has received a letter from Robert that is "nothing but Mrs. Pontellier from beginning to end." Robert has told Mademoiselle Reisz to play for Edna his favorite piece, the Impromptu of Chopin (the author's small joke).

Léonce Pontellier consults the family physician, Doctor Mandelet, about Edna (**chapter twenty-two**). "She's got some sort of notion in her head concerning the eternal rights of women; and—you understand—we meet in the morning at the breakfast table." Until this point in the story we have seen Edna's struggle as internal—psychological. The author has decided to set us straight, to supply a more obvious social and political frame for Edna's distress. The doctor responds accordingly, "[H]as she been associating of late with a circle of pseudo-intellectual women—super-spiritual superior beings? My wife has been telling me about them." Edna is not so easily categorized, however. She associates with no one. "[S]he goes tramping about by herself . . . getting in after dark," Léonce replies, "I tell you she's peculiar. I don't like it." The doctor advises him to leave Edna alone, that this may be just "some passing whim;" and anyway, a woman is "a very peculiar and delicate organism." The doctor privately suspects that another man may be the source of Edna's behavior.

Edna's father, the "Colonel" comes to New Orleans to buy a wedding gift for his other daughter, Janet, in **chapter twenty-three**. Edna and her father are not close, although they have "certain tastes in common." Edna sketches him. He takes her efforts most seriously, convinced that from him all his daughters have inherited "the germs of a masterful capability." It is his only charm. They attend a *soirée musicale* at Madame Ratignolle's where Mademoiselle Reisz plays. The little musician and the Colonel flirt, and Edna, herself "almost devoid of coquetry," marvels at the spectacle.

Doctor Mandelet dines with the Pontelliers a few days later. He observes Edna's behavior for signs of some secret she may be suppressing. Instead, he finds that there is "no repression in her glance or gesture." In fact, she reminds him of "some beautiful, sleek animal waking up in the sun." As part of the evening's entertainment Edna tells a story about a woman who leaves in a small boat with her lover one night, never to return. She falsely claims that Madame Antoine had related it to her: "Perhaps it was a dream she had had. But every glowing word seemed real to those who listened"—including the doctor. As he leaves the Pontelliers he regrets his practiced insight into the inner lives of people; he is weary of it. (Here the reader may perceive an authorial intrusion to notify us that this practiced insight may be best left to women novelists—such as Chopin.)

Edna and her father have an "almost violent" argument when she refuses to attend her sister Janet's wedding (**chapter twenty-four**). Her reasons are unknown to the reader; is Edna simply protesting the marriage? Following Doctor Mandelet's advice to allow Edna to do as she likes, Léonce refuses to intervene. The Colonel advises Léonce that he is too lenient with Edna; "Authority, coercion are what is needed. Put your foot down good and hard; the only way to manage a wife."

As if in imitation of Madame Ratignolle's domestic solicitude, Edna affectionately bids Léonce good-bye as he departs for New York on business. His mother takes the children to her home at Iberville, fearing that Edna might neglect them. Edna fully enjoys the "radiant peace" of her solitude. She assumes an easy authority over the servants, enjoys her dinner, thinks briefly and sentimentally about Léonce and the children, reads Emerson until she grows sleepy, and retires with "a sense of restfulness . . . such as she had not known before."

In **chapter twenty-five** Alcée Arobin emerges as "a familiar figure at the race course, the opera, the fashionable clubs." Charming, with a quiet though sometimes "insolent" manner, he is a frequent dinner companion for Edna. Arobin escorts Edna home on one such evening; she is restless, wanting "something to happen—something, anything; she did not know what." She regrets that she has not asked Arobin to stay and talk with her and she retires to a fretful sleep. A few days later Arobin calls upon Edna and the two spend the afternoon together at the races. Edna enjoys Arobin's easy charm and frank conversation. He shows her a dueling scar on his wrist; Edna impulsively clutches his hand as she examines the "red cicatrice," then draws away suddenly, sickened by it. The incident, with its sudden intimacy, "drew all [Edna's] awakening sensuousness." In response, Arobin feels impelled "to take her hand and hold it while he said his lingering good night." Edna is not unaware of the seductive nature of this encounter and she refuses to see Arobin again, though he insists that she allow him to return. Although Arobin is "absolutely nothing to her," the incident affects her "like a narcotic," and she retires to a "languorous sleep, interwoven with vanishing dreams."

The drama of the incident with Arobin embarrasses Edna in the "cooler, quieter moment[s]" of the following day (**chapter twenty-six**). Arobin sends a note of apology and comes to her home with "disarming naïveté." He adopts an attitude of "good-humored subservience and tacit adoration" in order to remain in her presence. In spite of her initial embarrassment, the candor of his speech appeals to "the animalism that stirred impatiently within her."

Edna visits Mademoiselle Reisz (**chapter twenty-six**) and announces that she intends to move out of her house into "a little four-room house around the corner. . . . I'm tired," she explains, "looking after that big house. It never seemed like mine, anyway—like home." Mademoiselle Reisz shrewdly discerns that Robert Lebrun is the cause of Edna's "caprice." She reveals to Edna that Robert is coming back to New Orleans. To complicate matters, and to put Edna's emotions into yet greater turmoil, Arobin kisses her the next evening (**chapter twenty-seven**), "the first kiss of her life to which her nature had really responded. It was a flaming torch that kindled desire." That night (**chapter twenty-eight**) she has an "overwhelming feeling of irresponsibility," disturbed that she experiences "neither shame nor remorse" over a kiss that did not signify love, but lust.

Edna begins feverish preparations to move into the little house (**chapter twenty-nine**), without waiting for a response to the letter she has sent her husband. Edna moves "everything which she had acquired aside from her husband's bounty" into the new house, "supplying simple and meager deficiencies" from the small allowance she receives from her mother's estate. Arobin visits her, perplexed and alarmed by her activities, but impressed at her "splendid and robust" appearance as she works alongside her housemaid. She assures Arobin that she will still give the dinner she has planned for two days hence. She tells him it will have "my best of everything" and wonders what Léonce will say when he pays the bills; Arobin wryly titles the event Edna's *"coup d'état."*

Edna's dinner party, on her twenty-ninth birthday, is a "small affair and very select" (**chapter thirty**). Among the guests are Arobin, Victor Lebrun, Mademoiselle Reisz, and Monsieur Ratignolle, Madame Lebrun and Adèle Ratignolle having characteristically sent their regrets. The table is "extremely gorgeous" and she wears a "cluster of diamonds that sparkled, that almost sputtered, in [her] hair," a present from her husband in New York. "[G]ood fellowship passed around [Edna and] the circle [of guests] like a mystic cord, holding and binding these people together with jest and laughter," until Victor, at the urging of the others, sings the song that Robert had sung to Edna in the boat that night from *Chênière*. Edna cries out that he must stop, shattering her wine glass "blindly upon the table." He does not take her protests seriously, however, until she moves behind him and covers his mouth with her hand. He kisses her hand and becomes quiet; Edna finds that the "touch of his lips was like a pleasing sting to her hand." In response to this intense display other guests "suddenly conceived the notion that it was time to say good night."

Arobin remains with Edna after the other guests depart (**chapter thirty-one**). He walks her home from the cottage, nicknamed "the pigeon-house." She is cold, miserable, and tired, as if "she had been wound up to a certain pitch—too tight—and something inside . . . had snapped." Arobin gently smoothes her hair and "[h]is touch conveyed to her a certain physical comfort. She could have fallen quietly asleep there if he had continued to pass his hand over her hair." He leaves only after Edna had become "supple to his gentle, seductive entreaties."

Stern correspondence from Mr. Pontellier, still in New York, expresses his "unqualified disapproval" of Edna's resolve to abandon her home (**chapter thirty-two**). To circumvent scandal he announces in the "daily papers . . . that their handsome residence on Esplanade Street was undergoing sumptuous alterations, and would not be ready for occupancy until their return [from a trip abroad]." Edna is impressed with his resourcefulness in the matter of public opinion. She is more pleased with the "intimate character" of her new home. After a brief visit to her children she is happy to return to the city, to be "again alone."

Edna meets Madame Ratignolle at Mademoiselle Reisz's apartment (**chapter thirty-three**) and learns that gossip has linked her romantically to Alcée Arobin. "Does he boast of his successes?" Edna asks, affecting disinterest. After Adèle departs, Mrs. Merriman and Mrs. Highcamp, named as if characters in a Restoration comedy, arrive and ask Edna to attend dinner and a game of "*vingt-et-un*" (Twenty-One). Arobin will take her home afterward, they tell her, and Edna accepts in a "half-hearted way."

Edna waits for Mademoiselle Reisz to arrive; she is stunned when Robert Lebrun appears at the door. They exchange small talk and Edna mistakenly believes that his feelings for her have changed. She decides to return home and Robert, "as if suddenly aware of some discourtesy in his speech," offers to escort her. She asks him what he has been "seeing and doing and feeling out there in Mexico." "[T]he waves and white beach of Grand Isle," he tells her, "the quiet, grassy street of the *Chênière*; the old fort at Grande Terre. . . . and feeling like a lost soul." He asks her the same question she has asked him, to which she gives the same reply; she, too, feels like "a lost soul."

Edna and Robert dine together at the pigeon-house, in **chapter thirty-four**. Their conversation becomes formal, with "no return to personalities." Afterward, once more alone, Edna is perplexed because he had "seemed nearer to her off there in Mexico" than he does in New Orleans. When she awakes the next morning (**chapter thirty-five**) Edna is certain that Robert loves her, and she regrets her "despondency" of the previous evening. She paints "with much spirit" for several hours, hoping that Robert will return; but three days later he has not. One night she goes riding with Arobin and they return to the little house to dine. His "delicate sense of her nature's require-ments like a torpid, torrid, sensitive blossom," evokes a response in Edna. Although she awakes the next morning without "despondency," she has lost all sense of "hope."

Chapter thirty-six opens in a garden in the suburbs of New Orleans. The garden, like Edna and her pigeon-house, is a "place too modest to attract the attention of people of fashion, and so quiet as to have escaped the notice of those in search of pleasure and dissipation." Edna's story is that of an ordinary woman. Later in the evening, Robert arrives unexpectedly. He admits that he left for Mexico to avoid her; he has been "fighting" his feelings for her since last summer at Grand Isle. Edna tells him that he had awakened her "out of a life-long, stupid dream." To add complication, Madame Ratignolle sends word that she is ill and asks Edna to come immediately. Robert begs Edna to stay there with him; she promises to return: "I shall come back as soon as I can; I shall find you here." The bedridden Adèle concludes chapter thirty-seven with a melo-dramatic plea to Edna that she "think of the children!"

Doctor Mandelet, aware of her distress over Madame Ratig-nolle's remark, walks Edna home (chapter thirty-eight): "You shouldn't have been there, Mrs. Pontellier," he said, "That was no place for you. Adèle is full of whims at such times. There were a dozen women she might have had with her, unimpres-sionable women. I felt that it was cruel, cruel. You shouldn't have gone." "I don't know that it matters after all," she responds, "One has to think of the children some time or other; the sooner the better." Doctor Mandelet is, apparently, a practitioner of the then new psychological precepts that would shape Freudian therapy. He urges Edna to consult with him at his office to "talk of things you never have dreamt of talking about before." Robert does not wait for Edna to return, but he leaves a note: "I love you. Good-by—because I love you." She remains awake all night.

In the final chapter of The Awakening Edna returns, alone, to Grand Isle, which is deserted until summer. Victor, making repairs, is describing to Mariequita the sumptuous dinner he attended at the Pontelliers, when both are stunned to see Mrs. Pontellier walking toward them from the dock. He offers her his room, since there "nothing fixed up yet." Edna tells them that she has come to rest, and to swim in the cold Gulf. In response to protests that the water is "too cold" to swim, Edna assures them that she will only "dip [her] toes in" and sends Mariequita to find her some towels. Her movements are mechanical; she notices nothing except that the sun is hot as she walks down to the beach. She has nothing more to think about now that Robert has abandoned her. In a paragraph that may be the key to the scandal this tale provoked when it was published, Edna reflects: "'To-day it is Arobin; to-morrow it will be some one else. It makes no difference to me, it doesn't matter about Léonce Pontellier—but Raoul and Etienne!' She understood now clearly what she had meant long ago when she said to Adèle Ratignolle that she would give up the unessential, but she would never sacrifice herself for her children." At the edge of the water, "absolutely alone," she takes off her clothes and, "for the first time in her life she stood naked in the open air . . . and the waves . . . invited her." As the water "enfold[s her] body in its soft, close embrace," she recalls her terror of being "unable to regain the shore" last summer, but now she thinks of a place she had known in childhood and which she thought "had no beginning and no end." Fatigue overwhelms her as she swims past the point of return, awakened to the magnitude of her unconscious self and unable to bear it. ✤

—*Tenley Williams*
New York University

List of Characters

Edna Pontellier, twenty-eight years old, is more handsome than beautiful, her face "captivating by reason of a certain frankness of expression and a contradictory subtle play of features." She is the daughter of a Civil War colonel of the Confederate army, raised in Kentucky and married, perversely because of the protests of her family, to a Creole New Orleans businessman, Léonce Pontellier. Her Protestant reserve contrasts with the risqué familiarity of the conversation of the married women in the Creole summer colony. Edna is without artifice and given to acts of "caprice," such as swimming beyond what others consider a safe distance from shore, acts which reflect her dissatisfaction with her unexamined, interior life. She is an "engaging" personality, neither very talented nor intellectually curious, and disinterested in Creole or any other domestic habits. In the space of a few months, she "awakens" to her "true" self. Hers is the "awakening" of an ordinary woman to love, the sensuous world, and her own spirituality. The ambiance of this social milieu at Grand Isle invites her to "loosen . . . the mantle of reserve that [has] always enveloped her," but Edna does not understand the rules of Creole society which, although they allow the language of personal freedom, demand as strict a propriety as any in the North. Hedonism, the pursuit of pleasure for its own sake, shapes her self-discovery, with disastrous results.

Léonce Pontellier is Edna's husband. He is forty-one years old, a slender, nearsighted, and unprepossessing Creole with a slight stoop. A prosperous New Orleans businessman, he is conventional, snobbish, kind, and generous to his wife and children, and emotionally remote. Edna's marriage to Léonce "was purely an accident, in this respect resembling many other marriages which masquerade as the decrees of Fate." In her inexperience and infatuation she had mistaken the flattery of his devotion for a "sympathy of thought and taste between them." Her Protestant family violently opposed her marriage to a Catholic which, the narrator tells us, was enough to ensure that she would marry him as quickly as possible. Léonce values Edna as he does all of his finest possessions.

Raoul and *Etienne* are Edna's two young sons. They interest her in "an uneven, impulsive way. . . . [S]he would sometimes forget them" entirely. Because they are in the constant company of their quadroon nursemaid, they cause no trouble and come to no harm, despite Edna's indifference.

Robert Lebrun is the instrument of Edna's "awakening" and the focus of her passion. The twenty-six-year-old son of Madame Lebrun, he devotes himself each summer to a young girl, widow, or married woman guest at Grand Isle, the summer colony on the Gulf of Mexico owned by his family. He is charming, idle, and in love with Edna Pontellier. Early one evening they swim together in the Gulf and Edna becomes aware of a "certain light [dawning] dimly within her,—the light which, showing the way, forbids it" (*chapter six*). He travels to Mexico in order to end their love affair; his reunion with Edna upon his return seems to fulfill her newly awakened desire. When he abandons her she commits suicide.

Alcée Arobin is a sophisticated and accomplished escort for respectable, married, New Orleans women of Edna's class. He frequently accompanies Edna to the horse races and to dinner when Léonce is away on business. His character both mirrors and contrasts Robert Lebrun. While Robert is in Mexico and Léonce is in New York, she succumbs to Arobin's practiced manner and approach. While he is attracted to Edna and not ungentlemanly in his conduct, his Creole sensuousness awakens her sexual passions, the passions she had focused upon Robert. Her feelings for Arobin confuse her and finally convince her that, without Robert, she will be only promiscuous.

Madame Adèle Ratignolle has been married seven years, has three children, talks constantly of her "condition," and has a fondness for candy. She has perfect hands. Edna, with her "sensuous susceptibility to beauty" is attracted by the physical charm and the personality of this Creole woman. She is a shrewd judge of the risks Edna takes in her love for Robert and in the appearance of an attachment to Alcée Arobin. In many ways, she acts as Edna's best friend. Edna often visits the Ratignolle's apartment, above their prosperous drugstore.

Mademoiselle Reisz is an elderly concert pianist. She is a single, disagreeable woman with no family and few friends. She is a symbol and an image of the life possible for an independent woman in 1899. While a guest at Grand Isle she develops a friendship with Edna and Robert. When Robert is in Mexico he writes letters to her about his love for Edna. Edna visits her apartment in New Orleans to read these letters from Robert.

Madame Lebrun is the mother of Robert and Victor. The summer colony of Grand Isle had been the luxury summer home of the Lebrun family. Madame Lebrun maintains her comfortable life by renting cottages to "exclusive visitors from the 'Quartier Francais'." Her efficiency and charm symbolize bourgeois Creole resourcefulness and respectability.

The Colonel is Edna Pontellier's father. He had been an officer in the Confederate army and is still known by his military title. He is gruff and opinionated, but he loves his daughter Edna. On a visit to New Orleans to buy a wedding gift for another daughter, he advises Léonce to be more firm with Edna, to allow her less freedom to neglect her domestic duties. Edna is happy to see him return to his Mississippi plantation.

Victor Lebrun is Robert's nineteen-year-old brother. He is youthfully infatuated with Edna, probably in response to the love his older brother feels for her. He is the last person to see Edna, at Grand Isle, before her suicide.

Doctor Mandelet is the kindly, paternal, and weary family physician to the Pontelliers and the Ratignolles. As an observer in the story he notes both her sad confusion and her ebullient charm. What he cannot understand, as Chopin illustrates, is that Edna's, or any woman's, dissatisfactions are rooted outside stereotypes of mental weakness. Although he is well-meaning, the good doctor is of little use to a woman.

Mrs. Merriman and *Mrs. Highcamp* are acquaintances of Edna in New Orleans. They function as stock characters in the story. They enjoy parties and horse racing in the company of Alcée Arobin, all the while maintaining their respectability as married women. Their names are reminiscent of characters in a late seventeenth-century comedy of manners. ❖

Critical Views

Percival Pollard (1869–1911) was a novelist and literary critic of the aesthetic-impressionist school. Pollard strove to gain an audience for many European works of literature and art in America. He is the author of a study of German drama, *Masks and Minstrels of New Germany* (1911). In the following extract, taken from Pollard's much celebrated *Their Day in Court* (1909), he comments on Edna's passion and captures some of the general impression of his day that the book was racy.

⟨. . .⟩ this seemed a subject for the physician, not the novelist. So skilfully and so hardily does the book reveal the growth of animalism in a woman, that we feel as if we were attending a medical lecture. In the old days,—when men, mere men such as Balzac or Flaubert or Gautier, attempted this sort of dissection,—we were wont to sigh, and think what brutes they must be to suppose women made of this poor clay. Surely it was only the males who harbored thoughts fit only for the smoking-room; surely—but, Pouff! Kate Chopin dispelled those dreams ⟨. . .⟩

"The Awakening" asked us to believe that a young woman who had been several years married, and had borne children, had never, in all that time, been properly "awake." It would be an arresting question for students of sleep-walking; but one must not venture down that bypath now. Her name was *Edna Pontellier*. She was married to a man who had Creole blood in him; yet the marrying, and the having children, and all the rest of it, had left her still slumbrous, still as innocent of her physical self, as the young girl who graduates in the early summer would have us believe she is. She was almost at the age that Balzac held so dangerous—almost she was the Woman of Thirty—yet she had not properly tasted the apple of knowledge. She had to wait until she met a young man who was not her husband, was destined to tarry until she was under the influence of a Southern moonlight and the whispers of the Gulf and many other passionate things, before there began in her the first faint flushings of desire. So, at any rate, Kate Chopin asked us to believe.

The cynic was forced to observe that simply because a young woman showed interest in a man who was not her husband, especially at a fashionable watering-place, in a month when the blood was hottest, there was no need to argue the aforesaid fair female had lain coldly dormant all her life. There are women in the world quite as versatile as the butterfly, and a sprouting of the physical today need not mean that yesterday was all spiritual.

However, taking Kate Chopin's word for it that Edna had been asleep, her awakening was a most champagne-like performance. After she met *Robert Lebrun* the awakening stirred in her, to use a rough simile, after the manner of ferment in new wine. *Robert* would, I fancy, at any Northern summer resort have been sure of a lynching; for, after a trifling encounter with him, Edna became utterly unmanageable. She neglected her house; she tried to paint—always a bad sign, that, when women want to paint, or act, or sing, or write!—and the while she painted there was "a subtle current of desire passing through her body, weakening her hold upon the brushes and making her eyes burn."

Does that not explain to you certain pictures you have seen? Now you know how the artist came to paint them just like that. ⟨. . .⟩

To think of Kate Chopin, who once contented herself with mild yarns about genteel Creole life—pages almost clean enough to put into the Sunday school library ⟨. . .⟩—blowing us a hot blast like that! Well, San Francisco, and Paris, and London, and New York had furnished Women Who Did; why not New Orleans?

"The black line of his leg moving in and out. . . ." Why, even that Japo-German apostle of plaquet-prose, Sadakichi Hartmann, did not surpass this when he wrote in his "Lady of the Yellow Jonquils": "She drew her leg, that was nearest to me, with a weavy graceful motion to her body. . . ."

It may seem indelicate, in view of where we left Edna, to return to her at once; we must let some little time elapse. Imagine, then, the time elapsed, and Robert returned. He did not know that Arobin had been taking a hand in Edna's awakening. Robert had gone away, it seems, because he scrupled to love Edna, she being married. But Edna had no scruples left; she hastened to intimate to Robert that she loved him, that her husband meant nothing to her. Never, by any chance, did she mention Arobin. But dear me, Arobin, to a woman like that, had been merely an incident; he merely happened to hold the torch. Now, what in the world do you suppose that Robert did? Went away—pouff!—like that! Went away, saying he loved Edna too well to—well, to partake of the fire the other youth had lit. Think of it! Edna finally awake—completely, fiercely awake—and the man she had waked up for goes away!

Of course, she went and drowned herself. She realised that you can only put out fire with water, if all other chemical engines go away. She realised that the awakening was too great; that she was too aflame; that it was now merely Man, not Robert or Arobin, that she desired. So she took an infinite dip in the passionate Gulf.

—Percival Pollard, *Their Day in Court* (New York: The Neale Publishing Company, 1909), pp. 40–42, 44

❖

KENNETH EBLE ON THE TRAGEDY OF EDNA'S SUICIDE

Kenneth Eble, a critic of American literature, is University Professor of English at the University of Utah, where he is head of the department. He is the author of *Howells: A Century of Criticism* (1962), *F. Scott Fitzgerald* (1963), and *Howells* (1984). In the following extract, Eble explores the tragedy of Edna's suicide and examines a letter from an enthusiast for the book.

Quite frankly, [*The Awakening*] is about sex. Not only is it about sex, but the very texture of writing is sensuous, if not sensual, from the first to the last. Even as late as 1932, Chopin's biographer, Daniel Rankin, seemed somewhat shocked by it. He paid his respects to the artistic excellence of the book, but he was troubled by "that insistent query—*cui bono*?" He called the novel "exotic in setting, morbid in theme, erotic in motivation." One questions the accuracy of these terms, and even more the moral disapproval implied in their usage. One regrets that Mr. Rankin did not emphasize that the book was amazingly honest, perceptive and moving. ⟨. . .⟩

It is a letter from an English reader which states most clearly, in a matter-of-fact way, the importance of Edna Pontellier. The letter was to Kate Chopin from Lady Janet Scammon Young, and included a more interesting analysis of the novel by Dr. Dunrobin Thomson, a London physician whom Lady Janet said a great editor had called "the soundest critic since Matthew Arnold." "That which makes *The Awakening* legitimate," Dr. Thomson wrote, "is that the author deals with the commonest of human experiences. You fancy *Edna's* case exceptional? Trust an old doctor—most common." He goes on to speak of the "abominable prudishness" masquerading as "modesty or virtue," which makes the woman who marries a victim. For passion is regarded as disgraceful and the self-respecting female assumes she does not possess passion. "In so far as normally constituted womanhood *must* take account of something *sexual*," he points out, "it is called love." But marital love and passion may not be one. The wise husband, Dr. Thomson advises, seeing within his wife the "mysterious affinity" between a married woman and a man who stirs her passions, will help her see the distinction between her heart and her love, which wifely loyalty owes to the husband, and her body, which yearns for awakening. But more than clinically analyzing the discrepancy between Victorian morals and woman's nature, Dr. Thomson testifies that Mrs. Chopin has not been false or sensational to no purpose. He does not feel that she has corrupted, nor does he regard the warring within Edna's self as insignificant.

Greek tragedy—to remove ourselves from Victorian morals—knew well *eros* was not the kind of *love* which can be easily prettified and sentimentalized. Phaedra's struggle with elemental passion in the *Hippolytus* is not generally regarded as being either morally offensive or insignificant. Mrs. Pontellier, too, has the power, the dignity, the self-possession of a tragic heroine. She is not an Emma Bovary, deluded by ideas of "romance," nor is she the sensuous but guilt-ridden woman of the sensational novel. We can find only partial reason for her affair in the kind of romantic desire to escape a middle-class existence which animates Emma Bovary. Edna Pontellier is neither deluded nor deludes. She is woman, the physical woman who, despite her Kentucky Presbyterian upbringing and a comfortable marriage, must struggle with the sensual appeal of physical ripeness itself, with passion of which she is only dimly aware. Her struggle is not melodramatic, nor is it artificial, nor vapid. It is objective, real and moving. And when she walks into the sea, it does not leave a reader with the sense of sin punished, but rather with the sense evoked by Edwin Arlington Robinson's *Eros Turannos*:

> . . . for they
> That with a god have striven
> Not hearing much of what we say,
> Take what the god has given;
> Though like waves breaking it may be,
> Or like a changed familiar tree,
> Or like a stairway to the sea
> Where down the blind are driven.

How wrong to call Edna, as Daniel Rankin does, "a selfish, capricious" woman. Rather, Edna's struggle, the struggle with *eros* itself, is farthest removed from capriciousness. It is her self-awareness, and her awakening into a greater degree of self-awareness than those around her can comprehend, which gives her story dignity and significance.

—Kenneth Eble, "A Forgotten Novel: Kate Chopin's *The Awakening*," *Western Humanities Review* 10, no. 3 (Summer 1956): 263, 267–69

❖

STANLEY KAUFFMANN ON THE SYMBOLIC USE OF THE SEA IN *THE AWAKENING*

> Stanley Kauffmann was an editor, actor, playwright, director, and critic of film, theater, and literature. He was the associate literary editor for *The New Republic*, editor-in-chief of Ballantine Books, and a theater critic for the *New York Times*. He is the author of *A World on Film: Criticism and Comment* (1966) and *Persons of the Drama: Theater Criticism and Comment* (1976). In the following extract, Kauffmann, after noting the similarities of *The Awakening* to Gustave Flaubert's *Madame Bovary*, explores the symbolism of the sea.

⟨. . .⟩ Like Emma Bovary, Edna Pontellier is an attractive young woman married to a well-meaning dullard, she is a mother, she is involved with two men, she commits suicide. Mrs. Chopin is not Flaubert's equal; her book does not have Flaubert's complexity of character or subtlety of orchestration; it lacks the breadth of context to make its intense anguish seem like an ironic winking moment in cosmic nonchalance; and there is no one scene in *The Awakening* that is conceived with the genius of such an episode as the one between Emma and Rodolphe at the agricultural fair. But there are two respects in which Mrs. Chopin's novel is *harder* than Flaubert's, more ruthless, more insistent on truth of inner and social life as sole motivation. Edna Pontellier has her first affair out of sexual hunger, without romantic furbelow. She is in love, but the young man she loves has left New Orleans (where most of the novel takes place). Increasingly aware that her life is increasingly empty, she has a sheerly sexual affair with an accomplished amorist. And, second, Mrs. Chopin uses no equivalent of the complicated financial maneuvers with which Flaubert finally corners his heroine. Edna kills herself solely because of the foredoomed emptiness of a life stretching ahead of her. It is purely a psychological motive, untouched by plot contrivance.

The patent them is in its title (a remarkably simple one for its day): the awakening of a conventional young woman to what is missing in her marriage, and her refusal to be content. Below that theme is the still-pertinent theme of the disparity between woman's sexual being and the rules of marriage. And below *that* is the perennial theme of nature versus civilization. The atmosphere of the book is that of frilled and formal New Orleans society (for, unlike Emma, Edna is not a provincial); but the book begins and ends with the sea.

It opens on Grand Isle in the Gulf of Mexico where the Pontelliers are summering, and it closes there. The very same sentence, about "the voice of the sea," occurs twice in the book. The first time, early in the story, is shortly after the following passage:

> Mrs. Pontellier was beginning to realize her position in the universe as a human being, and to recognize her relations as an individual to the world within and about her . . . perhaps more wisdom than the Holy Ghost is usually pleased to vouchsafe to any woman.

The sentence about the sea occurs once more, near the very end, just after the following:

> Despondency had come upon her there in the wakeful night, and had never lifted. There was no one thing in the world that she desired. There was no human being whom she wanted near her except Robert [the young man she loves]; and she even realized that the day would come when he, too, and the thought of him would melt out of her existence, leaving her alone. The children appeared before her like antagonists who had overpowered and sought to drag her into the soul's slavery for the rest of her days. But she knew a way to elude them. She was not thinking of these things when she walked down to the beach.

I submit that this is an extraordinary paragraph for an American novel published in 1899. It is neither Nora Helmer nor Susan B. Anthony. It is an anachronistic, lonely, existentialist voice out of the mid-20th century. ⟨. . .⟩

In the post-Freudian age, a certain patronizing view creeps into our reading of novels like this one, as if we thought that the author did very well considering that he didn't know as much about these matters as we do. An accompanying aspect is that we tend to give credit, even to Flaubert, on extra-literary grounds—pats on the head for being a pioneer. Still, after those aspects are either discounted or reckoned on, *The Awakening* remains a novel of high quality, fine in itself and astonishing for its day.

—Stanley Kauffmann, "The Really Lost Generation," *The New Republic* 155, no. 3 (December 3, 1966): 38

❖

CYNTHIA GRIFFIN WOLFF ON THE PSYCHOLOGICAL ASPECTS OF EDNA'S LIFE

Cynthia Griffin Wolff, author and literary critic, is an associate professor of English at the University of Massachusetts at Amherst. She is the author of *Samuel Richardson and the Eighteenth-Century Puritan Character* (1972). In the following extract, Wolff explores the psychological aspects of Edna's life.

Given the apparent terror which genuine emotional involvement inspires in Edna, her marriage to a man like Léonce Pontellier is no accident. No one would call him remarkable; most readers might think him dull, insensitive, unperceptive, even callous. Certainly he is an essentially prosaic man. If one assumed that marriage was to be an intimate affair of deep understanding, all of these qualities would condemn Léonce. Yet for Edna they are the very qualities which recommend him. "The acme of bliss, which would have been a marriage with the tragedian, was not for her in this world"; such bliss, indeed, is not for anyone *in this world*. It is a romantic allusion, a dream—defined by its very inability to be consummated. What is more, the intensity of dreams such as these may have become disturbing to Edna. So she chooses to marry Léonce; after all "as the devoted wife of a man who worshiped her, she felt she would take her place with a certain dignity in the world of reality, closing the portals forever behind her upon the realm of romance and dreams." The marriage to such a man as Léonce was, then, a defensive maneuver designed to maintain the integrity of the two "selves" that formed her character and to reinforce the distance between them. Her outer self was confirmed by the entirely conventional marriage while her inner self was safe—known only to Edna. An intuitive man, a sensitive husband, might threaten it; a husband who evoked passion from her might lure the hidden self into the open, tempting Edna to attach her emotions to flesh and blood rather than phantoms. Léonce is neither, and their union ensures the secret safety of Edna's "real" self. ⟨. . .⟩

If we try to assess the configuration of Edna's personality when she comes to Grand Isle at the novel's beginning, we might best do so by using R. D. Laing's description of the "schizoid" personality. As Laing would describe it, the schizoid personality consists of a set of defenses which have been established as an attempt to preserve some semblance of coherent identity. "The self, in order to develop and sustain its identity and autonomy, and in order to be safe from the persistent threat and danger from the world, has cut itself off from direct relatedness with others, and has endeavoured to become its own object: to become, in fact, related directly only to itself. Its cardinal functions become phantasy and observation. Now, in so far as this is successful, one necessary consequence is that the self has difficulty sustaining any *sentiment du réel* for the very reason that it is not 'in touch' with reality, it never actually 'meets' reality."

Laing's insights provide at least a partial explanation for elements of the novel which might otherwise be unclear. For example, Edna's fragility or susceptibility to the atmosphere at Grand Isle (as compared, for example, with her robust friend Madame Ratignolle, or the grand aloofness of Madame Reisz) can be traced to the circular ineffectiveness of the schizoid mechanism for maintaining identity. To be specific, such a person must be simultaneously alert to and protected from any invitation to interact with the real world since all genuine interactions leave the hidden "real" self exposed to potential danger. Vigilance begets threat which in turn precipitates withdrawal and renewed vigilance.

More important, interpersonal relationships can be conceived of only in cataclysmic terms; "there is a constant dread and resentment at being turned into someone else's thing, of being penetrated by him, and a sense of being in someone else's power and control. Freedom then consists in being inaccessible." Such habits of mind comport with Edna's outbursts concerning her own relationships. Certainly her rather dull husband seems not to notice her except as part of the general inventory of his worldly goods: thus early in the novel he is described as "looking at his wife as one looks at a valuable piece of personal property which has suffered some damage." Yet his attentions, such as they are, are rather more indicative of indifference than otherwise. Indeed, at every point within the narrative when he might, were he so inclined, assert his "rights," he declines to do so. After the evening swimming party, for example, when he clearly desires sexual intercourse and his wife does not wish to comply, he utters but a few sharp words and then, surprising for a man so supposedly interested in the proprietary relationship, slips on a robe and comes out to keep her company during her fitful vigil. After the return to New Orleans, he reacts to Edna's disruption of her "wifely functions" with but momentary impatience; he does not attempt coercion, and he goes to the lengths of consulting a physician out of concern for her well-being. Even when Edna has taken up residence in her diminutive "pigeon-house" Léonce decides to leave her to her own ways. His only concern—a small-minded one, to be sure—is to save appearances.

It is hard to cast such an ultimately insignificant man in the role of villain. ⟨. . .⟩ Léonce is a slender vehicle to carry the weight of society's repression of women. Yet Edna sees herself as his possession, even as she sees herself the prisoner of her children's demands. Her dying thoughts confirm this fixation: "She thought of Léonce and the children. They were a part of her life. But they need not have thought that they could possess her, body and soul." Now if Léonce is not able to rise to the occasion of possessing her body and soul, the children as they are portrayed in the novel, seem to exercise even less continuous claim upon her. They are always accompanied by a nurse whose presence frees Edna to pursue whatever interests she can sustain; what is more, they spend much of their time with their paternal grandmother, who seems to welcome them whenever Edna wishes to send them. Her emotional relationship with them is tenuous at best, certainly not demanding and by no stretch of the imagination stifling. "She was fond of her children in an uneven, impulsive way. She would sometimes gather them passionately to her heart; she would sometimes forget them." Given the extraordinary latitude that Edna did in fact have, we might better interpret her feelings of imprisonment as projections of her own attitudes and fears. The end of the novel offers an ironic affirmation of such a view, for when she returns home from Madame Ratignolle's accouchement, even her apparently positive expectations with regard to Robert follow the same familiar definition: "She could picture at that moment no greater bliss on earth than possession of the beloved one." The wording is somewhat ambiguous—she might possess him, he might possess her, the "possession" might be understood as a synonym for sexual union—still the key word here is *possession*, and it is Edna's word.

—Cynthia Griffin Wolff, "Thanatos and Eros: Kate Chopin's *The Awakening*," *American Quarterly* 25, no. 4 (October 1973): 452, 453–54

❖

Judith Fryer on Edna Pontellier's Childhood

Judith Fryer is a literary critic and the author of *Felicitous Space: The Imaginative Structures of Edith Wharton and Willa Cather* (1986) and *The Faces of Eve: Women in the Nineteenth Century American Novel* (1976), from which the following extract was taken. Fryer comments on Edna's awakening sense of separation from the people around her and examines references to Edna's childhood.

Even in her passive dream world ⟨. . .⟩ there is something unresolved about Edna in this marriage. "She is not one of us; she is not like us," Adèle Ratignolle, one of the women at Grand Isle, observes about her. Edna is unlike Madame Ratignolle, that "sensuous Madonna" with her "spun-gold hair that comb nor confining pin could restrain; the blue eyes that were like nothing but sapphires; two lips that pouted, that were so red one could only think of cherries or some other delicious crimson fruit in looking at them." Adèle is a fairy-tale heroine, but there is "no suggestion of the . . . stereotyped fashion-plate" about Edna. She is "different from the crowd" with her "long, clean and symmetrical" body, her quick and bright yellowish brown eyes, which she has "a way of turning . . . swiftly upon an object and holding them there as if lost in some inward maze of contemplation or thought." Edna's habit of introspection and her difference in appearance from other women suggest what is really different about her: she is not a "mother-woman." Mother-women prevail at Grand Isle; they are women who idolize their children, worship their husbands and esteem it "a holy privilege to efface themselves as individuals and grow wings as ministering angels." With these extended, protecting wings—very different from the kind of wings Edna will need to achieve her freedom—they flutter about their precious broods in the face of any harm, real or imaginary. The mother-woman, then, is one who thinks always about others, like Adèle Ratignolle, keeping up her music only for the sake of her family and cutting out patterns for her children's winter underwear in the middle of summer. Edna, on the other hand, thinks only of herself; she paints because she feels like painting and cannot "see the use of anticipating and making winter night garments the subject of her summer meditations." She explains to Madame Ratignolle on another occasion that she would never sacrifice herself for her children or for anyone: "I would give up the unessential; I would give up my money, I would give up my life for my children; but I wouldn't give up myself. I can't make it more clear; it's only something which I am beginning to comprehend, which is revealing itself to me." Edna's husband is unhappy that she is not more of a mother-woman; he reproaches her "with her inattention, her habitual neglect of the children," but he has been "a rather courteous husband so long as he met a certain tacit submissiveness in his wife." Once she has begun to awaken from her dream, however, her "new and unexpected line of conduct" completely bewilders and shocks him, and her "absolute disregard for her duties as wife" angers him. "She's got some sort of notion in her head concerning the eternal rights of women; and—you understand—we meet in the morning at the breakfast table," he finally complains to the doctor.

What has happened to Edna between the time Léonce regards her "inattention" with vague irritation and that when her "absolute disregard" angers him to the point where he cannot eat his food is Grand Isle and the sea. At Grand Isle Edna is awakened to a sense of herself as a person, rather than as a piece of valuable personal property. When she learns to swim, she becomes aware of the sensations of her body—the feel of the water against her limbs, the feel of the hot sun on her skin, the feel of the wind beating in her face; and with the awakened sense of her body comes sexual arousal. In her sexual desire for Robert, which she interprets as love, she is not unlike [Walt] Whitman's child on the beach. In fact, her awakening is a kind of rebirth of her childhood, and her love for Robert is similar to the fantasy-love she experienced before her marriage. Edna establishes the connection between her awakening and her renewed sense of childhood freedom in that final suicide scene. Standing naked in the open air she feels "like some new-born creature opening its eyes in a familiar world that it had never known." The sea makes her think of the "blue-grass meadow that she traversed when a little child," and the reader remembers another time, in the initial stages of her awakening, when the sea has reminded her of the blue-grass meadow. "I can trace . . . a meadow that seemed as big as the ocean to the very little girl walking through the grass, which was higher than her waist. She threw out her arms as if swimming when she walked, beating the tall grass as one strikes out in the water," she tells Madame Ratignolle. "I could only see the stretch of green before me, and I felt as if I must walk on forever . . . sometimes I feel this summer as if I were walking through the green meadow again; idly aimlessly, unthinking and unguided." As a child she walked through the meadow to escape her gloomy Presbyterian father; as a woman she walks into the sea first to escape her husband and then to escape all the antagonists who would drag her down— even Robert. Edna's awareness that it is not Robert, but her own awakening that has happened to her is clear when she tells him toward the end of the book, "You have been a very, very foolish boy, wasting your time dreaming of impossible things when you speak of Mr. Pontellier setting me free! I am no longer one of Mr. Pontellier's possessions to dispose of or not. I give myself where I choose. If he were to say, 'Here, Robert, take her and be happy; she is yours,' I should laugh at you both."

—Judith Fryer, *The Faces of Eve: Women in the Nineteenth Century American Novel* (New York: Oxford University Press, 1976), pp. 250–52

❖

JAMES H. JUSTUS ON THE SHORTCOMINGS OF EDNA PONTELLIER'S AWAKENING

> James H. Justus is an author and critic of American literature. He wrote *The Achievement of Robert Penn Warren* (1981). In the following extract, Justus questions just what Edna awakens to and if, in fact, her awakening is at all liberating.

What is it precisely which Edna Pontellier awakens *to*? It is clear what she awakens *out of*: the life of convention which denies her the full expression of all that is latent within her. The roles she plays in her life are defined not by her but by general circumstances, roles which though not heinous are merely conventional: dutiful wife, loving mother, gracious hostess, dependable friend. But in the course of her emotional and intellectual struggle, her new role—"free woman"—is never satisfactorily realized, and her specific lovers finally become as irrelevant as her friends, husband, and children.

Edna's awakening is neither sudden nor momentous. It begins, in fact, in childhood, during which time, Chopin tells us, Edna "lived her own small life all within herself. At a very early period she had apprehended instinctively the dual life— that outward existence which conforms, the inward life which questions." Significantly, it is not a passionate attachment to Robert Lebrun which first encourages the breakdown of the conforming patterns of her outward life, but *place*. It is setting, that most accentuated element of American local color fiction—setting in its larger sense—which serves that purpose.

Grand Isle, a Creole summer resort, is a place of languor, a place of hot sun enveloped by sea breezes from the Gulf, the place of Creole spontaneity and candor. Representing that society, momentarily displaced from a tropically luxuriant Gulf city to an even more tropically luxuriant island, is Adèle Ratignolle, the very epitome of the faithful Creole matron and presumably the one least likely to stimulate discontent within Edna. This "embodiment of every womanly grace and charm" does, however, strike a responsive chord in Edna, who has a "sensuous susceptibility to beauty." But though Adèle, like her sister Creole matrons, is marked by candor of speech, she is also like them, the very soul of fidelity. Attentiveness to husband, children, and home is so much the priority that it leaves no room for what Edna sees as a necessity—the inward life, an identity unconnected to matrimony. If these Creole women are characterized by an "entire absence of prudery" and a total freedom of expression which often embarrass the Kentucky Presbyterian, even Edna recognizes that "inborn and unmistakable" in them is a "lofty chastity" which can not be compromised. In a rare editorializing note, Chopin wryly calls these Grand Isle matrons "mother-women . . . , fluttering about with extended, protecting wings when any harm, real or imaginary, threatened their precious brood. They were women who idolized their children, worshipped their husbands, and esteemed it a holy privilege to efface themselves as individuals and grow wings as ministering angels."

If Adèle Ratignolle is one kind of foil for Edna Pontellier, Mademoiselle Reisz is quite another kind. This "disagreeable little woman, no longer young," with a self-assertive temper and a "disposition to trample upon the rights of others," quarrels with everyone at Grand Isle and is so visibly distressed by its general domestic flavor that one wonders how she can possibly endure so homogenous a watering place. And if Adèle grows wings as a ministering angel, Mademoiselle Reisz knows something about other kinds of wings. After her return to the city, Edna cultivates Mademoiselle Reisz, visiting her, reading Robert's letters, listening to appropriate piano music. At the end of one of these visits, Mademoiselle Reisz puts her arms around Edna and feels her shoulder blades to see if "her wings were strong." "The bird that would soar above the level plain of tradition and prejudice must have strong wings," she says. "It is a sad spectacle to see the weaklings bruised, exhausted, fluttering back to earth." Although Edna professes to be thinking of no "extraordinary flights," the final natural object she sees before her suicide in the Gulf is a "bird with a broken wing . . . beating the air above, reeling, fluttering, circling disabled down, down to the water." ⟨. . .⟩

For Adèle, complacent satisfaction—never being alone—comes from having no identity beyond her given roles; for Reisz, the ambiguous satisfactions of having her own identity is the result of always being alone. Relentlessly anti-domestic, Reisz is bored and annoyed by children. Adèle lives only for them. At the very moment Edna seems destined to begin her affair with Robert, she is called to Adèle's bedside where the matron is giving birth to yet another child and where, at the end of her labor, she whispers to Edna, "Think of the children, Edna. Oh think of the children. Remember them!" The injunction comes many months after the Grand Isle summer, where in a confiding moment Edna had declared to Adèle that she would never sacrifice herself for her children: "I would give up the unessential; I would give my money, I would give my life for my children; but I wouldn't give myself."

Edna is caught between the claims of "mother-women" and those of "artist-women," between the sensual aspects of Creole women, who adjust to society by celebrating their procreative powers, and the brittle independence of liberated artists, who resist their culture's sociological limitations with their own kind of creative powers. There is little comfort for Edna in either Madame Ratignolle or Mademoiselle Reisz, despite the fact that between these two she unconsciously vacillates, instinctively seeking a model for her own inchoate longings for an identity lying somewhere unformulated and undefined. There is only herself as she gropes for clarification of what she wants. It is not surprising that Kate Chopin's original title for *The Awakening* was "A Solitary Soul." The evidence suggests that the powerful drive toward freedom, to that state where her real identity can be released from the confines of social roles, is the impetus behind Edna's sensual groping and blundering. Neither friends nor lovers can release that identity, and the tragedy within the novel is that even Edna Pontellier, despite her emotional changes, cannot release that identity.

—James H. Justus, "The Unawakening of Edna Pontellier," *The Southern Literary Journal* 10, no. 2 (Spring 1978): 108–11

❖

Linda Huf on the Greek Concepts of Thanatos and Eros in *The Awakening*

> Linda Huf is a literary scholar and critic of American literature. She is the author of *A Portrait of the Artist as a Young Woman: The Writer as Heroine in American Literature* (1983), from which the following extract was taken. Huf comments on the presence of Thanatos and Eros in *The Awakening*.

[Edna Pontellier] confesses to [Doctor Mandelet] that she is a woman who wants her own way and regrets that, in order to get it, she has had to "trample on the lives, the hearts, the prejudices of others." Still, she "shouldn't want to trample on the little lives." But she doesn't want to think of the children now, either hers and Léonce's or, if nature takes its course, hers and Robert's. She means "to think of them . . . but not tonight." Tonight, she anticipates the greatest "bliss on earth"—the "possession of the beloved one." "To-morrow would be time to think of everything." But when she enters her cottage she discovers that the beloved one has absconded. She stretches herself out on the sofa and until the morning light she thinks—of the children.

When the next day, back on Grand Isle, she walks to her death in the sea, she is not thinking of anything in particular. She has done all her thinking the night before when she lay awake upon the sofa. First she thought of Robert, and realized that "the day would come when he, too, and the thought of him would melt out of her existence, leaving her alone." Passionate love, as Doctor Mandelet had suggested, is an illusion, and a transient one at that, guaranteed only to remain long

47

enough to leave behind children, of whom one must think ever after. Indeed, the transience of erotic love is a *leitmotif* that runs through the novel. Everywhere Edna turns on Grand Isle she sees an old woman in black creeping closely behind a pair of nameless young lovers who have eyes only for each other. It is an image, of course, of Thanatos stalking Eros, of the death of love pursuing all young lovers, Edna and Robert not excepted. Had Edna obtained her heart's desire—the "possession of the beloved one"—nature would have assured that her ecstasy last only long enough to bring her to childbed. Sexual love, as Doctor Mandelet had said, is a decoy designed by nature to secure mothers for the race.

Thus, Edna thought the night before about the transience of sexual love, but she also thought about the permanence of what it gives rise to: the children, and one's responsibility to them. She thought: "To-day it is Arobin; to-morrow it will be someone else." She did not care about the effect of her awakening on her husband, but she did care about its effects on Raoul and Etienne.

> Her children appeared before her like antagonists who had overpowered her and sought to drag her into the soul's slavery for the rest of her days. But she knew a way to elude them.

For the first time Edna clearly understands what she meant long ago when she told Adèle that she would give up the unessential, including her life, for her children, but she would never sacrifice the essential; that is, her very being. She would never, and she does not. She goes to her death in order not to have to renounce—for the sake of her children—her newly awakened self, including the newly awakened sensuality that has become an important part of her and without which she would be but a fragment of a complete human being.

We see, then, that throughout the novel Edna has wavered between two influences, that of the artist Mademoiselle Reisz and that of the mother-woman Madame Ratignolle. The artist advises her to acquire the "courageous soul," the "soul that dares and defies." The mother-woman advises her to "remember the children." The two messages are contradictory. Edna cannot dare and defy convention at the same time she must remember the children. She cannot realize herself, let alone her talent, as long as she is unwilling to see her children suffer for her behavior. Although Edna is in fact that something new under the sun—the New Woman, which all the newspapers were talking about—she still lives in an "old" society, with its old conventions, prejudices, and superstitions. It is obvious that there is no place for the New Woman in *fin de siècle* America, nor is there a suitable mate for her. As Edna herself realizes, Robert "did not understand. He would never understand." He had wanted her to leave off being one of Mr. Pontellier's possessions and become one of his own. The truth is that Edna is alone, and alone she is too small a David to fell the Goliath of convention. In isolation her battle can only fail. This important fact was suggested graphically in the scene in which Edna threw down her wedding ring and stamped on it, but her boot heel was too little to make even the slightest mark. Edna's lonely awakening to herself—to her sensual, imaginative, and artistic potential—must fail because in a society which refuses to recognize her primary "position in the universe as a human being," but sees her only as a woman—that is, as a wife and mother—she cannot realize herself, let alone her gift, unless she is willing to disgrace those closest to her: her children. And Edna is not willing.

—Linda Huf, *A Portrait of the Artist as a Young Woman: The Writer as Heroine in American Literature* (New York: Frederick Ungar, 1983), pp. 77–79

❖

ROSEMARY F. FRANKLIN ON THE MYTH OF PSYCHE AND EDNA PONTELLIER

Rosemary F. Franklin, a critic of American literature, teaches English at the University of Georgia. In the following extract, taken from "The Awakening and the Failure of Psyche," Franklin retells the myth of Psyche and argues that Edna can be read as a Psyche figure.

Despite the intense critical attention Kate Chopin's *The Awakening* has received in the last fifteen years, it is still not clear whether Edna Pontellier is a hero or victim. One recent reader sees her suicide as a "defiant act of will" and another as a result of "maternal longing." A reading of the novel is possible which mediates the extremes of Edna as either tragic or pathetic. The Eros and Psyche myth is a useful pattern to illuminate the labor toward self of the female hero with the accompanying inner and outer threats to the attainment of selfhood.

Several commentators have noted the irony of the title. Edna sleeps and lives in a world of romantic fantasy far more than she seems to awaken to self or reality. The magnetic Gulf of Mexico beckons her to a world of dreams and then destruction. Freudian and other psychological critics have helpfully detailed the infantile and regressive traits in Edna, but this line of inter-pretation tends to view Edna's struggle as narrowly patholog-ical rather than universally human. If, however, we view Edna as a Psyche figure, it is more clear that heroism is necessary for the nascent self to resist the lure and power of the uncon-scious.

Psyche's story is that recurring one of the mortal who arouses the antagonism of the gods. Aphrodite is jealous that her subjects have turned from her to worship the beautiful Psyche. The goddess condemns the girl to marriage with a monster, but her son Eros has conceived a passion for the mortal and spirits her away to a palace where she is provided with all luxuries and he visits her anonymously. Aroused by her jealous step-sisters to suspect her lover is truly a monster, Psyche aggressively decides to see him and kill him. As she holds a lamp over him, however, she sees Eros, the beautiful god, and startled by this knowledge, she burns him with lamp oil; simultaneously she is wounded by one of his arrows. Eros then flees because she has broken her promise to love him unseen. When Aphrodite hears of this liaison, she retaliates with a series of labors for Psyche: a chaotic pile of seeds to sort, golden wool to be stolen from raging rams, water to be fetched from high mountain springs. The tasks seem so impos-sible to Psyche that, during the course of these labors, she has two impulses to commit suicide. But emissaries from nature help her in the work she cannot finish alone.

In her last and most hazardous task, she is instructed by Aphrodite to confront death itself by going to Hades to fetch a beauty ointment from Persephone. Again, Psyche thinks of suicide, believing it is the only way to the underworld, but a speaking tower tells her a shortcut and warns her not to weaken her resolve by stopping along the way to show pity to those who ask her aid. On her way home, however, Psyche succumbs to her desire to use some of the ointment to attract Eros. Its application brings on a deep and death-like sleep. Moved by her act to please him, Eros forgets his mother's prohibition and rushes to save her by removing the ointment. In the happy conclusion, Psyche is elevated to the realm of the immortals, they marry, and the child Joy is born.

Most commentators view this ancient tale as a myth of psychic growth. In recent years Erich Neumann has led historically with his Jungian analysis of 1952. With other approaches follow Bruno Bettelheim, Lee Edwards, Rachel Blau DuPlessis, and Mary Ann Ferguson, some with controversy over whether this myth is only about feminine development, as Neumann asserts. All of these critics agree, however, that Psyche's struggle with unconscious powers is the core of the tale. The jealous Aphrodite, appearing in the myth as the Terrible Mother, fears the threatening growth of mortal consciousness. The collective, here occurring as a matriarchy, can manifest itself either as social pressure or as the seductive lure of the unconscious. The emerging self must set itself against both. Psyche's passive life in the dark palace with Eros is not possible after she lights her lamp, sees him, and wounds him and herself. Separation and solitude test her resolve for individuation and, along with the difficulty of the tasks, threaten to overwhelm her. Psyche's attempts at suicide mark these impulses to return to unconscious passivity. Edna Pontellier experiences all of Psyche's difficulties and more as she makes her way through both sexual and self awakenings. The paradigm of the myth illuminates the significant action, characters, and symbols of her complex, psychological struggle.

—Rosemary F. Franklin, "*The Awakening* and the Failure of Psyche," *American Literature* 56, no. 4 (December 1984): 510–12

♣

BONNIE ST. ANDREWS ON THE ROLE OF THE PONTELLIER
CHILDREN IN *THE AWAKENING*

> Bonnie St. Andrews, a literary critic, is the author of
> *Forbidden Fruit: On the Relationship Between Women
> and Knowledge in Doris Lessing, Selma Lagerlöf, Kate
> Chopin, and Margaret Atwood* (1986), from which the
> following extract was taken. St. Andrews explores the
> role of Edna's children in *The Awakening.*

⟨. . .⟩ the children in *The Awakening* merit—as is absolutely the
case with children—attention. Children are keys to their parents' characters; through James and Cam, Mrs. Ramsay is
revealed [in Virginia Woolf's *To the Lighthouse*] and through
Paul Morel, Gertrude Coppard Morel [in D. H. Lawrence's *Sons
and Lovers*]. And surely the offspring of Leonce and Edna Pontellier embody their parents' personalities.

Leonce and Edna are erratically attentive; both parents seem
now loving, now laissez-faire. What is of particular significance
seems, of course, the question of whether a non-"mother-
woman" causes emotional or personal damage in her children.
The children of such a woman (and of a "man's man"), Etienne
and Raoul, seem hearty, unspoiled, and positively independent. They are leaders of the other, one might almost say, over-
weaned children.

The children of Leonce and Edna Pontellier share the bon-
bons with other children, pick themselves up when they fall,
receive hugs and reprimands with equanimity. Under pressure
of peers these brothers combine; they "Usually prevailed
against the other mother-tots." So Chopin, through these many
children, distinguishes mother-women from Edna but also
"mother-tots" from Edna's children. And neither women nor
children seem to suffer damages through diversity.

This attitude toward laissez-faire mothering techniques
might, given the Victorian credo that the "angel in the house"
must be and wants to be at every moment responsive to the
children or to the husband, have seemed threatening to
Chopin's 1899 readership. Certainly, critics deplored Edna Pontellier's refusal to act the part of the "mother-woman" who

"idolized their children, worshipped their husbands, and esteemed it a holy privilege to efface themselves as individuals and grow wings as ministering angels."

And if Edna Pontellier is no "mother-woman," Leonce Pontellier is surely no "father-man." Chopin introduces Leonce amidst a domestic cacophony of parrots and children and sewing machines; he attempts to read the financial section of an old newspaper. His response to children and domestic choirs is comparable to that of W. C. Fields. Yet what besides "mother love" could excuse the Farival twins? All the guests hear, entirely too often and at unsettling volume, their rousing rendition of "Zampa" which so torments Leonce Pontellier. Yet Leonce is hardly dismissable as a comic character.

Leonce Pontellier is a complex, decent male who finds himself quite suddenly faced with opposition. He is a businessman of considerable reputation, dedicated to preserving and observing, as he puts it, "le convenances." But as spokesman for the status quo, Leonce is neither buffoon nor tyrant; he is, rather, a responsible Victorian husband and father who, having contracted a perfectly suitable arrangement with Edna, finds her changes puzzling.

Precisely because Edna and Leonce Pontellier have managed their marriage so well—with its divisions of labor and of interest—Edna's leaving must have startled the 1899 readership. Certainly Leonce is praised and praised lavishly by the wives on Grand Isle. His enterprises thrive and expand; he shares this bounty with wife and children. The other wives pronounce Leonce Pontellier "the best husband in the world" to which, with characteristic restraint, Edna Pontellier "was forced to admit that she knew of none better."

Both principals in this marriage—as in the union of the Ratignolles—know their roles and their responsibilities. Edna and Adele contract fine marriages; these characters and their unions serve as foils for Chopin, through which male and female variety is observed. The husbands are successful, mannerly men who expect emotional support and unquestioning obedience from their wives. These couples represent, to the Marxist critics, the practical arrangement outlined by Engels as that of the propertied classes. In such unions, the wife-mother becomes a decorative or aesthetic object with only limited uses and plays proletariate to the male's bourgeoisie. Or, as Veblen might put it, the female becomes the model and showcase of the male's social/fiscal power. The banquet scene, Edna's birthday party, testifies not only to Edna's leaving such great luxury but also to Leonce's success in the material world.

—Bonnie St. Andrews, *Forbidden Fruit: On the Relationship Between Women and Knowledge in Doris Lessing, Selma Lagerlöf, Kate Chopin, and Margaret Atwood* (Troy, NY: The Whitson Publishing Company, 1986), pp. 43–45

❖

Barbara C. Ewell on the Outsider in Creole Culture

Barbara C. Ewell is a professor of English at Loyola University in New Orleans, Louisiana. She is the author of *Louisiana Women Writers* (1991) and *Kate Chopin* (1986), from which the following extract was taken. Ewell looks at the tropical sensuality evoked in the setting of *The Awakening* and the role of the outsider in Creole culture.

Edna's recollection, for the first time since childhood, of her romantic dreams and the pleasures of the senses is profoundly related to her milieu. Chopin freely evokes the rich atmosphere of New Orleans and Grande Isle, drenching the novel with the "light and languor" (Ch. 2) of summer days and soft breezes, the seductive odors and sounds of the Gulf. Even when Edna returns to the city, it is "the soft, gusty beating of the hot south wind" (Ch. 19) and the images of Grande Isle that haunt her imagination and stir her emotions. This lush setting creates both a physical motive for Edna's behavioral changes and a resonant metaphor for the fervid sensuality those changes reflect.

Chopin couples this tropical sensuality with another theme familiar in her work: the outsider in Creole culture. A Protestant from the upper South, Edna is, like David Hosmer, "not thoroughly at home in the society of Creoles." Their "entire absence of prudery" is rather startling: she listens with shock and embarrassment to the risqué stories and detailed accounts of childbirth told in mixed company; she is astonished to find a racy novel openly discussed. That such freedom is accompanied by "a lofty chastity" is a paradoxical heritage of the Creoles' Catholic and European roots that Chopin had exploited in "Two Portraits." Secure in their Catholic convictions about the indissolubility of marriage and the adequacy of maternity for feminine fulfillment, the Creoles can afford the liberty of indecorous speech and a superficial physical intimacy. The unshakable reality of chastity is never threatened, and indeed, seems protected by these outlets. As an outsider—an American—whose Puritan legacy is a distrust of the body, Edna is unprepared for this lax environment that calls into question her own customary reserve. With its superficial freedoms, this alien culture, reinforced by the sensory stimulation of the Gulf, provides what has been called "a climate of psychological relaxation" and the initial impulse for Edna's awakening.

But while these elements loosen Edna's repressions, they do not channel her energies in any specific way. Since the age of twelve when, she recalls, "religion took a firm hold upon" her, Edna has lived reflexively, "just driven along by habit." As these defining habits now slip away, she experiences a vague anguish, an unthinking aimlessness, to which she responds with impulse and caprice: refusing and then accepting Robert's invitation to the beach, later going out on her day for receiving guests, or moving to the pigeon house. As is often the case in Chopin (*cf.* Mrs. Sommers, Archibald, or Graham), such disorientation signals a critical transition, the chaos preceding insight.

The particular catalyst of Edna's reorientation is Robert. A romantic given to flirtatious poses with unavailable women, Robert embodies the unsatisfied passions of Edna's youth. His presence also focuses the sensuality disguised by her romantic dreams. Through Robert, Edna tentatively experiences the possibility of venturing beyond the prescribed patterns of her life. Not coincidentally, the sexual tension in their flirtation is revealed the very evening Edna learns to swim, a crucial image of her efforts at selfhood. Having failed all summer to master this art, Edna is one night like a "little tottering, stumbling, clutching child, who of a sudden realizes its powers, and walks for the first time alone, boldly and with over-confidence." Her new-found control immediately tempts Edna to excess, swimming "far out, where no woman had swum before." As Paula Treichler observes, the passage, with its implied warnings of premature confidence, pinpoints both the spiritual dimensions and sexual-political risks of Edna's act. And anticipating her final swim as well as her experimental rejection of her former life, Edna's elation is immediately succeeded by a "quick vision of death," mirroring the inexperience and lack of strength that later undermine her efforts at selfhood.

—Barbara C. Ewell, *Kate Chopin* (New York: Ungar Publishing Company, 1986), pp. 146–48

❖

DALE M. BAUER ON EDNA'S SEARCH FOR A LANGUAGE OF SELF-EXPRESSION

Dale M. Bauer is a literary critic with a special interest in women writers. He is the author of *Edith Wharton's Brave New Politics* (1995). In the following extract, taken from *Feminist Dialogics: A Theory of Failed Community* (1988), Bauer discusses Edna's search for a language with which she can express her specifically feminine desires.

⟨. . .⟩ Chopin's novel simultaneously articulates the socializing norms of the Creole community and the conflicting gendered voices. She plays on the typical encoding of woman-as-mother in her relation to the hero; in fact, Chopin turns this romantic structure on its head, creating in Edna's fragmented voice a denial of the ideologeme of the mother-woman. Her voice's fragmented, halting quality testifies to the strength of the cultural code, the very ideology of motherhood and creativity Edna contests. Chopin plays out this feminine difference in the orchestration of voices in *The Awakening*.

One of Edna's first realizations about the tradition she has internalized occurs for her when she understands how she has been constructed as subject of a particularly American ideology. About the "Subjective 'I'" Joanne Frye states: "To speak directly in a personal voice is to deny the exclusive right of male authority implicit in a public voice and to escape the expression of dominant ideologies upon which an omniscient narrator depends." That Edna has come to speak for her personal will is the subject of many feminist readings of Chopin; how she does so—and the political consequences of the ideologeme of self—is the subject of this chapter.

Edna realizes that she fills the gaps of others' desires for her: as Léonce Pontellier's possession; as Dr. Mandelet's medical enigma; as Adèle's mother-woman; as Mlle. Riesz's struggling artist. As far as these others are concerned, Edna has no desires of her own. Chopin, however, gives birth to Edna's voice, which in turn gives birth to feminine desires as they are constructed through her battle with Creole culture. Edna wants to feel and articulate desire as private property, as a language to which she has access. The production of this female subjectivity emerges out of the opposition between Edna's dissatisfaction and the Creole culture's reification of woman-as-sign. In Edna, the contradictions—internalized and hated—she hears in her own head emerge before she can come to know her own desires. 〈. . .〉 Edna wants an imaginary totality of self, a coherent self, but must respond to contradictory expectations of her—that she live for the children, for her husband and other "fathers," for the Creole notion of wife. In short, her self does not exist, having been fractured into fragments and shards of her own desire.

What Edna wants is a selfhood not tied to reciprocal love, sexual passion, the responsibility of children. That Edna only has the language of romantic love and sexual passion—and no language of a specifically feminine desire at that—is the ground of the struggle. Thus, her desires are limited no longer by her husband and children and friends alone—the community which fails her—but by the patriarchal tongue which is not at all a "mother tongue" and which she cannot refashion to fit her own linguistic intentions.

—Dale M. Bauer, *Feminist Dialogics: A Theory of Failed Community* (Albany, NY: State University of New York Press, 1988), pp. 129–31

❖

ELIZABETH FOX-GENOVESE ON CHOPIN'S VIEW OF WOMEN'S LIBERATION

Elizabeth Fox-Genovese teaches at Emory University. She contributed *"The Awakening* in the Context of the Experience, Culture, and Values of Southern Women" to *Approaches to Teaching Kate Chopin's "The Awakening."* Fox-Genovese argues that Chopin's novel was not intended to make a broad social statement but rather that it indicates that Chopin viewed women's independence as a personal matter.

Life in the postbellum South intensified the explicit identification of the tight relations between gender, class, and race relations. Southern suffragists varied in degree, but not in substance, on their analysis of the necessary link between women's rights and the racial balance of their society: they concurred that the woman's vote should not be allowed to increase the black vote. Chopin did not participate in the heated discussions about women's rights, which she surely viewed as yet another side of the social question. But aspects of her work strongly suggest that she sought, as it were, to write around or above the issue. Neither *The Awakening* nor any of her other writings suggest that she secretly espoused woman suffrage or related causes. To the contrary, everything that she wrote, including *The Awakening*, indicates that she viewed women's independence as a personal more than a social matter. In one moving passage, she does imply that her own independence derived in no small measure from the deaths of her husband and her mother—that is, from her release from social constraints as embodied in those she loved. Passages in *The Awakening* even suggest that she recognized children as a possible fetter on women's self-determination, although she never otherwise hinted that she felt so about her own. But the constant, underlying current in her writings makes it clear that she took no inconsiderable pride in having attained a sophisticated and independent maturity on her own, within the limitations that her society imposed. In *The Awakening*, she carefully delineates both the possibility for women's happiness within marriage (Mme Ratignolle) and the possibility for their independence from it (Mlle Reisz).

Strange as it may seem to modern readers, there is reason to believe that Chopin intended her explorations of women's sexual self-awareness to pose less of a threat to the social order of her world than explorations of their social independence would have. In this respect, her attitudes represent a stark reversal of those of [Charlotte Perkins] Gilman, as manifested in the two women's attitudes toward doctors. For Gilman, the doctor constituted a kind of political vanguard and buttress of the husband, understood as oppressor. For Chopin, he constituted a wise confidant who fully appreciated the complexities of woman's nature. Chopin's open discussion of women's sexuality proved, in the event, to shock her southern contemporaries as profoundly as her northern ones. The South, after all, remained too American. Even the veneer of New Orleans local color—and all southerners accepted New Orleans as different—and of Chopin's self-conscious European style did not protect her. Chopin may not fully, or more to the point consciously, have known what she was risking, but she did know what she was attempting.

Chopin's sympathy for women's personal and sexual independence sank its roots in a tragic view of the human condition derived from a Catholic sensibility that persisted long after Chopin had abandoned regular Catholic practice. This view of human nature resulted in the notion that personal matters should be personal, should not challenge the social order. Chopin's preoccupation with European naturalism only reinforced her inherited sense of how original sin and established social relations pressed on the individual's internal and external possibilities for freedom. Edna ultimately fails in her bid for freedom because she lacked the personal strength to recognize the difference between the contingent and the essential. Chopin gambled on presenting woman's nature as a universal problem. She set her sights on Aeschylus and Shake-speare, not on Ibsen. She may have thought that her attempt to treat sexuality independent of gender relations respected the social values of southern society, but she misjudged.

In *The Awakening*, Kate Chopin self-consciously sought to move beyond the specific southern identification of her local-color stories. She surely did not intend her novel as a specific reflection of the values of southern women, parochially defined. Yet today, the novel gains resonance if read and taught in historical context. As a novelist, Chopin navigated between specificity of detail and universality of theme. It is difficult not to wonder if she fully understood how firmly that strategy linked her to the emerging modern tradition of southern let-ters. No social or domestic novelist, she wrote of the female human condition as a full member of that distinctive culture which would also inform the work of William Alexander Percy and William Faulkner.

—Elizabeth Fox-Genovese, "*The Awakening* in the Context of the Experience, Culture, and Values of Southern Women," *Approaches to Teaching Chopin's "The Awakening,"* ed. Bernard Koloski (New York: The Modern Language Association of America, 1988), pp. 38–39

❖

Peggy Skaggs on Literary Naturalism in *The Awakening*

Peggy Skaggs, a critic of American literature, teaches at Angelo State University. She contributed "*The Awakening*'s Relationship with American Regionalism, Romanticism, Realism, and Naturalism" to *Approaches to Teaching Chopin's "The Awakening."* Skaggs applies the theories of literary naturalism to *The Awakening*.

During the 1890s, naturalism became an important literary mode in America. The tendency toward naturalism is clear enough in *The Awakening* to enable students to grasp its basic deterministic philosophy, as Edna finds that her life must be lived within socioeconomic and biological boundaries as unyielding as the walls around any penitentiary.

Edna's first act of rebellion—and the beginning of the end of her relationship with Léonce—is her refusal to hold her usual reception day for people important to Léonce's business. Her friendships are expected to contribute to her husband's success. In fact, the romantically charming Creole society dictates that its women find all their satisfactions through wifehood and motherhood. It produces ideal mother-women like Adèle Ratignolle but forbids women to develop any other talents or interests. Although Mlle Reisz creates beautiful music on the piano, everyone despises her. The neighborhood grocer declares that he is thankful she has left the neighborhood; although Reisz is the only genuine musician the Ratignolles know, they never invite her to their musical soirees; even Edna often finds Reisz offensive. No one in the entire novel ever addresses the pianist by her first name, if indeed she even has one. And as soon as Edna begins trying to develop her own ability to paint, Léonce accuses her of neglecting her family. Procreation should be enough creativity to satisfy any woman. Edna's social life and personal development are thus circumscribed by socioeconomic forces as powerful as those that control the life of [Theodore] Dreiser's Sister Carrie, for example, or of any other naturalistic protagonist.

Biology has also helped to determine Edna's destiny. When nature made her female, it established the rhythm of her life, a subtle but important point that Chopin makes by structuring the novel around Adèle's pregnancy. And the inescapable pain of Adèle's childbirth as well as Edna's overwhelming love for Raoul and Etienne result at least in part from the women's biological nature. Motherhood enchains women in *The Awakening* through a combination of pain and love. Although Edna's sons play only minor roles in the novel, they nevertheless control her destiny and lead her to suicide. Many students dismiss Edna's declaration that she is taking her life because of her love for Raoul and Etienne, because they feel that she has exhibited little warmth toward the boys throughout the story. But such judgmental attitudes tend to fade when students understand Edna's social milieu and the naturalism in the novel.

⟨. . .⟩ This novel can be viewed as both a product and a climax of nineteenth-century American literary tendencies. Regionalism and romanticism predominated in the earlier nineteenth century—and in the setting and plot of *The Awakening*. Romanticism yielded after the Civil War to an antiromantic impulse that resulted in the psychological and social realism of [Henry] James, [William Dean] Howells, and [Mark] Twain; similarly, the romantic setting and plot of *The Awakening* become antiromantic as they stifle Edna and prevent her expansion as a person. Before the turn of the century, naturalism was emerging with its focus on biological and socioeconomic determinism; and Edna's tragedy is that she yearns to live fully, to fly high above tradition and all limitations to her personhood—yet finds her flight blocked at every turn by biological and social limitations.

> —Peggy Skaggs, "*The Awakening*'s Relationship with American Regionalism, Romanticism, Realism, and Naturalism," *Approaches to Teaching Chopin's "The Awakening,"* ed. Bernard Koloski (New York: The Modern Language Association of America, 1988), pp. 83–84

❖

MICHAEL T. GILMORE ON THE SIMILARITIES BETWEEN THE IMAGERY OF *THE AWAKENING* AND THE IMPRESSIONIST SCHOOL OF PAINTING

Michael T. Gilmore is a professor of English at Brandeis University and a literary scholar who concentrates on eighteenth- and nineteenth-century American writers. He is the author of *The Middle Way* (1977) and *American Romanticism and the Marketplace* (1985). In the following extract, Gilmore argues that the lush imagery and setting of *The Awakening* is similar to that of the Impressionist school of painting.

Chopin thoroughly immerses Edna's story in the upper-middle-class world of the late nineteenth century. The exquisite, detailed rendering of life among the affluent is what gives the book its distinctive texture, and Edna's growing sense of entrapment does not prevent her from taking pleasure in many aspects of leisure-class existence. Events unfold against a backdrop of elegant homes and secluded resorts. Chopin's writing conveys the sensual richness of these settings, as in her description of the beach at Grand Isle, reached by sandy paths among acres of yellow camomile and glistening clumps of orange and lemon trees; or her account of the table setting for Edna's dinner party, with its profusion of red and yellow roses, "cover of pale yellow satin under strips of lace-work," and "wax candles in massive brass candelabra, burning softly under yellow silk shades" (Chap. 30). Since a good part of the action occurs during the long summer vacation on the Gulf, people are shown amusing themselves at activities like swimming, strolling on the beach, attending musical *soirees*, and taking excursions to exotic islands. Servants, seemingly always colored, are everywhere, from the quadroon who looks after the Pontellier boys on Grand Isle, to the cook who spoils Leonce's soup in New Orleans, to the black woman, Old Celestine, who accompanies Edna to the pigeon house and prepares her meals for her.

⟨. . .⟩ The lush, sensuous ambience of Chopin's novel is notably similar to that of the world portrayed in Impressionist paintings of two or three decades earlier. The resemblance extends both to subject matter and technique. Meyer Schapiro has commented on "how many pictures we have in early Impressionism of informal and spontaneous sociability, of breakfasts, picnics, promenades, boating trips, holidays and vacation travel." Canvases like [Edouard] Manet's *Déjeuner sur l'herbe* (1863) and [Georges] Seurat's *A Sunday Afternoon on the Island of La Grande Jatte* (1884-6) strongly evoke Chopin's work. Chopin also suggests the Impressionists in her interest in creating atmosphere through sensory imagery, particularly color and light. From the first sentence, she flecks her pages with vivid dabs of paint. Like Edna, whose love of sunbathing so exasperates her husband, the book's prose seems "to be one with the sunlight, the color, the odors, the luxuriant warmth of some perfect Southern day" (Chap. 19).

More telling than these surface affinities is the deeper kinship between Edna's evolving state of mind and the objectives of Impressionist art. Rather than aspiring to an unmediated vision of reality, Impressionism is concerned with a given scene's effect on the individual consciousness; by giving priority to the sensations of the artist, it actively disfigures or decomposes the external world. Shapes tend to lose their solid form as they change and blur in accordance with the shifting position or feelings of the observer. The spontaneous is preferred to the static, the momentary accorded a higher value than the permanent. Schapiro asserts that Impressionism's "unconventionalized, unregulated vision" implies "a criticism of symbolic social and domestic formalities, or at least a norm opposed to these." So understood, Impressionist painting can be viewed as the aesthetic analogue to Edna's jettisoning of religion, family, and community as a result of her awakening. Outer reality in the novel undergoes a radical destabilization as she yields to passing sensations and becomes increasingly prey to moods. Chopin writes that "she was seeing with different eyes and making the acquaintance of new conditions in herself that colored and changed her environment" (Chap. 14). Unwilling to suppress her emerging self, she begins "to do as she liked and to feel as she liked" (Chap. 19). In responding to the demands of her inner nature, Edna discovers the sensibility of an Impressionist painter and dissolves the external structures of her world.

Where Edna and the Impressionists most agree, then, is in their common turning inward, their transfer of allegiance from the outer world to the personality and freedom of the individual. For the Impressionists, this transfer involved a partial emancipation from the authority of natural forms. As [Paul] Cézanne put it, "I have not tried to reproduce Nature. . . . Art should not imitate nature, but should express the sensations aroused by nature." But though Impressionism is part of the general trend in modern art toward abstraction and the primacy of inner feelings, it remains bound to recognizable objects such as haystacks and water lilies; its break with representation is incomplete. Edna and Chopin are ultimately unable to transcend the Impressionist compromise, yet they nonetheless strive to go beyond it and to achieve something approximating the modernist escape from everyday reality. Both women wish to find a way out of the "fettering tradition of nature," and both aspire to speak, like the brightly colored parrot introduced on the novel's first page, "a language which nobody understood."

—Michael T. Gilmore, "Revolt Against Nature: The Problematic Modernism of *The Awakening*," *New Essays on "The Awakening*," ed. Wendy Martin (New York: Cambridge University Press, 1988), pp. 63, 64–65

❖

ANDREW DELBANCO ON EDNA PONTELLIER'S LACK OF OWNERSHIP AND SENSE OF IDENTITY

Andrew Delbanco, a scholar of American literature, is a professor of English at Columbia University. He is the author of *The Puritan Ordeal: Becoming American in the Seventeenth Century* (1988). In the following extract, Delbanco examines Edna's lack of ownership in Chopin's novel and reads this in specifically Marxian language and analysis, such as the "alienation" experienced by the dispossessed.

⟨. . .⟩ Chopin has used a teasing sentence of possible irony to mark the moment of the novel's shift from the open spaces of Grand Isle to the interiors of New Orleans: "The Pontelliers possessed a charming home on Esplanade Street." The force of this sentence, it turns out, lies in the fact that it is not ironic at all. Edna has become an equal partner in its plural subject—a possessor too. She has, in other words, begun to escape the condition of being (or at least learning to be) a Creole woman. But it is not sufficient to speak of what she has left behind. To come fully to terms with this novel, we must confront the terrible limbo into which Edna now falls. By the time of Leonce's departure, *The Awakening* has become a book about her suspension not merely between Kentucky Presbyterianism and Creole Catholicism, or between halves of the city divided by Canal Street, but between the genders themselves.

It is a transformation that has been hinted from the start. "She was rather handsome than beautiful," we are told early, and before long she learns to drink "liquor from the glass as a man would have done." This most basic of the novel's suspensions—between the feminine and the masculine as forms of social being—takes a predictably large psychic toll. Edna's statement that "I am beginning to sell my sketches," for instance, is a check on her emerging artistic commitment, which is explicitly associated with female dissent from the male world of commodity display and exchange. Surely her moment of highest self-realization comes when she is able—as no one else is save Madame Ratignolle (with her children) and Mademoiselle Reisz (with her music)—to take pleasure in the intrinsic value of something she has produced: "She had reached a stage [with her painting] where she seemed to be no longer feeling her way, working, when in the humor, with sureness and ease. And being devoid of ambition, and striving not toward accomplishment, she drew satisfaction from the work in itself." In Chopin's world, at least, this is an experience unavailable, or, more accurately, unaffordable, for men. Edna's brush with it is one of those moments when it is useful to think of *The Awakening* in roughly Marxian terms; she has done nothing less than make an escape from alienation. Even if it is only a fleeting freedom, she conceives, for a moment, of neither her work nor herself as a commodity—which is why "I am beginning to sell my sketches" is double-edged. What in one sense is a tremor of professionalism—a feminist victory—is also a lapse into equating the expression of self with goods and services whose value depends on social use. Both aspects of Edna's awakening—the liberating and the constricting—are adumbrated in the brilliant account of her father's visit: Once a proud colonel in the Confederate army, now an astringent minister, he sits "before her pencil . . . rigid and unflinching, as he had faced the cannon's mouth in days gone by." This is, if ever there was one, a phallic pencil; an emblem of daughterly usurpation. As both Mademoiselle Reisz and Madame Ratignolle begin to realize, Edna is replacing her thralldom to particular men—father, husband, imagined lovers—with the thrill of partaking in exactly the experience that they had once monopolized: the experience of power.

⟨. . .⟩ Edna is learning a new language of impulse that is, at least within the universe of the novel, explicitly identified as female, and this is precisely why it is so ominous when she falls back into the mimicry of men: "I hardly think we need new fixtures, Leonce. Don't let us get anything new: you are too extravagant. I don't believe you ever think of saving or putting by." Such uxorious language is a fair imitation of Leonce's nagging; Edna is wavering, insecure in her new self, beginning to notice that her new "feminine" discourse flusters the men around her. And so she relents, making her fatal compromise. The captive is learning to emulate the captor.

It should be said that Edna's "awakening" never wholly renovates her consciousness. She "never awakens," as one critic points out, "to the dimensions of her social world . . . never sees how the labor of the mulatto and black women around her makes her narcissistic existence possible." Because of the servitude of others, she is able to keep the world of her children at a muted distances: "The boys were being put to bed; the patter of their bare, escaping feet could be heard occasionally, as well as the pursuing voice of the quadroon." The children's life upstairs is all very abstract to Edna, a bit of background noise. She exists in a relation to governess and children that is not very different from her husband's. Even childbirth itself is something she had once barely apprehended through an anesthetic haze. ⟨. . .⟩ [Leonce] and Edna, we begin to realize, are not so much an opposition as a matched pair, a symmetry that Chopin carefully evokes by balancing the opening chapter with the last: Our first sight of Leonce comes as he watches his wife emerge from the sea; we watch with him, feeling his isolation as she twines into intimacy with Robert beneath the "pink-lined shelter" of her sunshade; then, at the other end of the book, we watch Edna walk back into the sea and feel that first moment echoed—if reversed.

—Andrew Delbanco, "The Half-Life of Edna Pontellier," *New Essays on "The Awakening,"* ed. by Wendy Martin (New York: Cambridge University Press, 1988), pp. 98-99, 100–101

♣

Mary E. Papke on Edna Pontellier's Childhood Memories

Mary E. Papke is an assistant professor of English at the University of Tennessee and assistant editor of the journal *Literature and Psychology*. She is the author of *Susan Glaspell: A Research and Production Sourcebook* (1993). In the following extract, taken from *Verging on the Abyss: The Social Fiction of Kate Chopin and Edith Wharton* (1990), Papke explores the significance of Edna's awakening memory of childhood.

Edna continually positions herself near the sea in the Grand Isle sequence [of *The Awakening*] so that the sea washes over her senses at all times; as occurs in the sense experiences of the solitary souls in the short stories [of Kate Chopin], it functions both as a projection and reflection of her desire. What it reveals to her is that she cannot lead the dual life of Adèle, cannot be a true woman who wilfully sublimates self-desire in self-effacing service to others: "In short, Mrs. Pontellier was beginning to realize her position in the universe as a human being, and to recognize her relations as an individual to the world within and about her." Chopin also indicates that this movement of quickening consciousness cannot be anything but "vague, tangled, chaotic, and exceedingly disturbing" and that, again, process instead of singular revelation is all.

That Edna has from early on been predisposed to pursuing the individual, or exceptional, rather than the socially determined, or sanctioned, life is shown in her childhood remembrances: "Even as a child she had lived her own small life all within herself. At a very early period she had apprehended instinctively the dual life—that outward existence which conforms, the inward life which questions." In other words, she has always been both susceptible to the sensuous and intuitively aware of her own circumscribed female existence. Her awakening, however, comes only after intellectual apprehension of what her feelings intimate. First, Edna's attraction to Adèle's beauty and Adèle's sympathetic response to Edna's tentative self-disclosures encourage Edna to explore the continuum of her existence, the past out of which comes her present and on which her future is predicated. Shortly after her confrontation with Léonce, Edna and Adèle sit alone by the sea. Edna stares into the water, and in answer to Adèle's question about her inwardness, she consciously explores the maze of her inner contemplation: "'I was really not conscious of thinking of anything; but perhaps I can retrace my thoughts.'" The sea has made her recall another "sea" of her childhood: she thinks of "a summer day in Kentucky, of a meadow that seemed as big as the ocean to the very little girl walking through the grass which was higher than her waist. She threw out her arms as if swimming when she walked, beating the tall grass as one strikes out in the water." Edna further recalls her childhood awareness of self-limitation: "'My sun-bonnet obstructed the view. I could see only the stretch of green before me, and I felt as if I must walk on forever, without coming to the end of it.'" More importantly, she understands the connection of that self to her present, how her horizons are yet limited and her desire for unobstructed vision bewildering: "'sometimes I feel this summer as if I were walking through the green meadow again; idly, aimlessly, unthinking and unguided.'" Adèle's response is to enclasp Edna's hand, an affectionate but ultimately futile sign of feminine empathy toward the womanhood condition. This first caress, however, serves to provoke Edna's further self-exploration; the sensuous, even in small ways, leads to self-realization and denial of blind, mechanical, or nonreflective behavior.

Edna begins then to analyze for the first time the past, the history of her self-constitution, and she perceives the bases for her self-alienation in her childhood's lacks—her motherlessness and her father's coldness—as well as in her propensity for romantic self-delusion. Her infatuation with unattainable men, most notably and ironically that with a famous tragedian, a man who acts out emotionally, and her business alliance with Léonce only furthered her sense of irrevocable duality: the split between inward and outward expression, her desires set in conflict with social expectations. She had, like so many women, effected the sublimation of her self-will and knowledge by rationalizing the unrealizability of passion, coming to believe that the most life could offer her was passive adoration. ⟨. . .⟩ So too did she take on the role of mother, "a responsibility which she had blindly assumed and for which Fate had not fitted her." It is only at the age of twenty-eight, with Adèle by the sea, that she admits to the dark side of such self-capitulation, that to be a wife and mother is, for some, only another denial of self-responsibility. She is, however, despite the concern and show of affection from Adèle and Robert, alone with this realization, and she cannot as yet take her intuitions a step further toward self-consciousness until inspirited once more by the sensuous embrace of the sea.

> —Mary E. Papke, *Verging on the Abyss: The Social Fiction of Kate Chopin and Edith Wharton* (Westport, CT: Greenwood Press, 1990), pp. 73–75

❖

BERT BENDER ON CHARLES DARWIN'S THEORIES AND *THE AWAKENING*

Bert Bender, a scholar of American literature, teaches English at Arizona State University. He is the author of *Sea Brothers: The Tradition of American Sea Fiction from Moby-Dick to the Present* (1988). In the following extract, Bender relates Charles Darwin's theories, as expressed in *The Descent of Man* (1871), to *The Awakening*.

⟨. . .⟩ Edna's response to Mademoiselle Reisz's piano performance of a piece by Frédéric Chopin is clearly based on a passage from Darwin, the point of which is that music was originally the means by which our "half-human ancestors aroused each other's ardent passions" ([*The*] *Descent* [*of Man*], II, 337).

Edna had responded to music before, but never as she will during this performance. Before, music had sometimes evoked in her a picture of "solitude" that is again a measure of Chopin's passage beyond [Walt] Whitman's mid-nineteenth-century view of life. She had imagined "the figure of a man standing beside a desolate rock on the seashore. He was naked. His attitude was one of hopeless resignation as he looked toward a distant bird winging its flight away from him" (chap. 9). Even in this echo from [Whitman's poem] "Out of the Cradle Endlessly Rocking," the "hopeless resignation" of Chopin's man presents a considerably darker view of life and solitude than that projected by Whitman. Still, in this image of a "distant bird winging its flight away," there is a suggestion of the consoling thought which Whitman had imagined in the surviving he-bird's song, or in the solitary thrush's in "When Lilacs Last in the Dooryard Bloom'd." But this image had come to Whitman's "awakened" imagination in "Out of the Cradle" (in 1859), and when Edna fully awakens to Chopin's view of the Darwinian reality by the end of the novel, the bird will reappear as the image of the spirit defeated—"with a broken wing . . . beating the air above, reeling, fluttering, circling disabled down, down to the water" (chap. 39).

The musical performance on August twenty-eighth is crucial in propelling Edna toward her final bleak awakening, for here her response to the music is as Darwin explained in *The Expression of Emotions:* music can cause a person to "tremble," to feel "the thrill or slight shiver which runs down the backbone and limbs," or to experience "a slight suffusion of tears" that resembles "weeping" caused by other emotions. Thus, during this musical performance in *The Awakening*, "the very first chords which Mademoiselle Reisz struck upon the piano sent a keen tremor down Mrs. Pontellier's spinal column." And because "her being was tempered to take an impress of the abiding truth," she finds that "the very passions themselves were aroused within her soul, swaying it, lashing it, as the waves daily beat upon her splendid body. She trembled, she was choking, and the tears blinded her" (chap. 9). The musical performance moves others, too: "What passion!" one exclaims—"It shakes a man!" Immediately following the performance the group decides to take a midnight swim; and now, like a joyful child taking her first steps, Edna realizes that she can swim. Feeling that "some power of significant import had been given her to control the workings of her body and soul," she wants to "swim far out, where no woman had swum before" (chap. 10). Later, alone with Robert, she tells him of the "thousand emotions" that had swept through her as a result of Mademoiselle Reisz's playing, and before they part she is "pregnant with the first-felt throbbings of desire."

Chopin indicates at once that Edna's developing desire will eventually lead her into "abysses of solitude." when she enters the water on this night, she gathers "in an impression of space and solitude" from "the vast expanse of water"; and in her solitary swim she realizes that she might perish "out there alone." Moreover, the simultaneous development of her desire and her sense of solitude will eventually lead her to a clearer understanding of her "position in the universe" as an animal and therefore as a creature empowered to participate fully in the sexual reality as a self-conscious selector (chap. 6). Her development toward claiming the power to select is gradual, but she takes a first crucial step immediately after her swim by refusing to yield to Mr. Pontellier's "desire." And a few days later she awakens more fully to her animal nature after fleeing from an oppressive church service to Madame Antoine's seaside home. Here, awakened from a nap, "very hungry," she "bit a piece" from a loaf of brown bread, "tearing it with her strong, white teeth" (chap. 13).

⟨. . .⟩ Clearly, Edna's strong teeth indicate her kinship with our "half-human ancestors" in *The Descent of Man*, for she tells Robert that the "whole island seems changed" now: "a new race of beings must have sprung up, leaving only you and me as past relics" (chap. 13).

—Bert Bender, "The Teeth of Desire: *The Awakening* and *The Descent of Man*," American Literature 63, no. 3 (September 1991): 467–68, 469

❖

ELAINE SHOWALTER ON GUY DE MAUPASSANT'S INFLUENCE ON KATE CHOPIN

Elaine Showalter is a noted literary critic and professor of English at Princeton University. She is the author of *A Literature of Their Own: British Women Novelists from Brontë to Lessing* (1976) and *The Female Malady: Women, Madness, and English Culture, 1830-1980* (1985). In the following extract, taken from *Sister's*

Choice: Tradition and Change in American Women's Writing (1991), Showalter places *The Awakening* in the context of other American novels of its day and examines the influence of the stories of Guy de Maupassant.

In contrast to [Louisa May Alcott's] *Little Women*, embraced from the moment of its publication to the present by unbroken generations of readers, Kate Chopin's *The Awakening* (1899) has been a solitary book. Generally recognized today as the first aesthetically successful novel to have been written by an American woman, it marked a significant epoch. *The Awakening* broke new thematic and stylistic ground as Chopin went boldly beyond the work of her precursors in writing about women's longing for sexual and personal emancipation. Yet the novel represents a literary beginning as abruptly cut short as the heroine's awakening consciousness. Edna Pontellier's explicit violations of the modes and codes of nineteenth-century American society shocked contemporary reviewers, who condemned the book as "morbid," "essentially vulgar," and "gilded dirt." Banned in Chopin's home town of St. Louis, and censured in the national press, *The Awakening* dropped out of sight and remained unsung by literary historians and unread by several generations of American writers.

In the early stages of her career, Chopin had tried to follow the literary advice and literary examples of others, and had learned that such dutiful efforts led only to imaginative stagnation. By the mid-1890s, when she came to write *The Awakening*, Chopin had come to believe that the true artist was one who defied tradition, who rejected both the *convenances* of respectable morality, and the conventions of literary success. When, as she was "emerging from the vast solitude in which I had been making my own acquaintance," she encountered a story by [French author Guy de] Maupassant called "Solitude,"she recognized a kindred soul: "Here was a man who had escaped from tradition and authority, who had entered into himself and looked out upon life through his own being and with his own eyes." This is very close to what happens to Edna Pontellier as she frees herself from social obligations and received opinions and begins to "look with her own eyes; to see and to apprehend the deeper under current of life."

Chopin was also moved by Maupassant's melancholy affirmation of human separateness, when he wrote, "Whatever we may do or attempt, despite the embrace and transports of love, the hunger of the lips, we are always alone." To a woman who had survived the illusions that friendship, romance, marriage, or even motherhood would provide lifelong companionship and identity, and who had come to recognize the existential solitude of all human beings, Maupassant's declaration became a kind of credo. ⟨. . .⟩ Much as she admired Maupassant, and much as she learned from translating his work, Chopin felt no desire to imitate him. Her belief in originality and autonomy in writing is expressed by Mademoiselle Reisz, the musician in *The Awakening*, who tells Edna that the artist must possess "the courageous soul that dares and defies" and must soar above "the level plain of tradition and prejudice."

None the less, even in its defiant solitude, *The Awakening* belongs to a historical moment in American women's writing, and Chopin could not have written without the legacy of domestic fiction to write against, and the models of the local colorists and New Women writers with which to experiment. After the Civil War, the homosocial world of women's culture began to dissolve as women demanded entrance to higher education, the professions, and the political world. The female local colorists who began to publish stories about American regional life in the 1870s and 1880s were also attracted to the male worlds of art and prestige opening up to women, and they began to assert themselves as the daughters of literary fathers as well as literary mothers. Claiming both male and female aesthetic literary models, they felt free to present themselves as artists and to write confidently about the art of fiction in essays like Elizabeth Stuart Phelps's "Art for Truth's Sake." Among the differences the local colorists saw between themselves and their predecessors was the question of "selfishness," the ability to put literary ambitions before domestic duties. Although she had been strongly influenced in her work by Harriet Beecher Stowe's *Pearl of Orr's Island*, Sarah Orne Jewett came to believe that Stowe's work was "incomplete" because she was unable to "bring herself to that cold selfishness of the moment for one's work's sake."

Writers of this generation chose to put their work first. The 1870s and 1880s were what Susan B. Anthony called "an epoch of single women," and many unmarried women writers of this generation lived alone; others were involved in "Boston marriages," or long-term relationships with another woman. But despite their individual lifestyles, many speculated in their writing on the conflicts between maternity and artistic creativity. Motherhood no longer seemed to be the motivating force of writing, but rather its opposite. Thus artistic fulfillment required the sacrifice of maternal drives, and maternal fulfillment meant giving up artistic ambitions.

—Elaine Showalter, *Sister's Choice: Tradition and Change in American Women's Writing* (New York: Oxford University Press, 1991), pp. 65–67

❖

LYNDA S. BOREN ON MADEMOISELLE REISZ'S INFLUENCE ON EDNA PONTELLIER

Lynda S. Boren has lectured at various colleges and universities. She received a Fulbright lectureship for the University of Erlangen-Nuremberg, Germany, and one for Srinakharinwirot University, Bangkok, Thailand. She is the author of *Eurydice Reclaimed: Language, Gender and Voice in Henry James* (1989). In the following extract, Boren examines the influence of Mademoiselle Reisz and her piano playing on Edna.

With each visit to Reisz's apartment, we notice a change in Edna. At her first, "the little musician laughed all over when she saw Edna." She takes Edna's hand "between her strong wiry fingers, holding it loosely without warmth, executing a sort of double theme upon the back and palm." In this first visit, Reisz aggressively manipulates Edna, withholding a letter from Robert Lebrun until she has Edna under her influence. Quoting from the letter, Reisz recalls Robert's words: "'If Mrs. Pontellier should call upon you, play for her that impromptu of Chopin's, my favorite. I heard it here a day or two ago, but not as you play it. I should like to know how it affects her.'" Reisz produces the letter only after Edna begs to hear the impromptu. As Edna reads the letter, Reisz begins to play a soft interlude, an improvisation, her body settling into ungraceful curves and angles that give it an appearance of deformity. Reisz's body is possessed by a grotesque will (ugly, demonic) that overrides any concern for Edna's well-being. Gradually and imperceptibly, the interlude melts into the soft opening minor chords of the Chopin impromptu. At the end of this session, Reisz picks up the letter, crumpled and damp with Edna's tears. She smoothes the letter out, restores it to the envelope, and replaces it in her table drawer.

Shortly thereafter, Mr. Pontellier consults Dr. Mandelet about Edna's behavior. "'Has she,' asked the Doctor, with a smile, 'has she been associating of late with a circle of pseudo-intellectual women—super-spiritual superior beings? My wife has been telling me about them.' . . . 'That's the trouble,' broke in Mr. Pontellier, 'she hasn't been associating with any one. She has abandoned her Tuesdays at home, has thrown over all her acquaintances, and goes tramping about by herself, moping in the street cars, getting in after dark. I tell you she's peculiar. I don't like it; I feel a little worried over it.'"

However, Edna's determination to perfect her artistry during this period of delicious solitude is weakened by some deep absence or loss in her life that overcomes her. Only Reisz's music has the power to free her soul. After a disappointing evening with friends, Edna returns home to prepare a solitary feast. In the preparation of this repast, Edna begins to take on the witchlike characteristics of Reisz, as though she were indeed possessed. "She rummaged in the larder and brought forth a slice of 'Gruyere' and some crackers. She opened a bottle of beer which she found in the icebox. Edna felt extremely restless and excited. She vacantly hummed a fantastic tune as she poked at the wood embers on the hearth and munched a cracker." ⟨. . .⟩

During Edna's second visit, Reisz gives her a letter from Robert that she has secreted under a scowling bust of Beethoven. This time, Edna does not begin at once to read Robert's letter; she listens first to Reisz's music "She sat holding the letter in her hand, while the music penetrated her whole being like an effulgence, warming and brightening the dark places of her soul. It prepared her for joy and exultation." In this intense encounter, Edna seems to get the better of Reisz, however. Her love for Robert is too strong a spell even for the witchery of Reisz. ⟨. . .⟩

Edna's reunion with Robert, as might be expected, takes place in Reisz's apartment. By this point, Edna has begun to pluck at the piano as if to summon up on her own the magic that had first inspired her. "Edna seated herself at the piano, and softly picked out with one hand the bars of a piece of music which lay open before her. A half hour went by. There was the occasional sound of people coming and going in the lower hall. She was growing interested in her occupation of picking out the aria, when there was a second rap at the door." One glance from Robert, however, dispels the enchantment of music. ⟨. . .⟩

So much has transpired in Edna's life since Robert's departure, so fatal has Reisz's touch been to her spirit, however, that a life with Robert is now impossible. As Edna witnesses the torture of Ratignolle's childbirth, the awakening alluded to might not only inform the title of Chopin's work (which she agreed to change from *A Solitary Soul*) but also signify Edna's final realization that nothing, not even Robert, can fulfill the longing of her soul. ⟨. . .⟩ Edna swims away to solace, away from the painful passions that had enslaved her, even those inspired by Reisz's music. "She thought of Leonce and the children. They were a part of her life. But they need not have thought that they could possess her, body and soul." The final images attending Edna's drowning, especially that of the chained dog, offer an ironic contrast to her will to freedom.

—Lynda S. Boren, "Taming the Sirens: Self-Possession and the Strategies of Art in Kate Chopin's *The Awakening*," *Kate Chopin Reconsidered*, ed. Lynda S. Boren and Sarah de Saussure Davis (Baton Rouge, LA: Louisiana State University Press, 1992), pp. 192–94

❖

JOYCE DYER ON THE SYMBOLIC USE OF THE PARROT IN THE
OPENING OF *THE AWAKENING*

> Joyce Dyer is an assistant professor of English and
> director of the writing program at Hiram College in
> Hiram, Ohio. She has written many articles on Kate
> Chopin and other American authors. In the following
> extract, taken from *The Awakening: A Novel of Begin-
> nings* (1993), Dyer explores the significance of the
> parrot in the first lines of *The Awakening*.

A green and yellow parrot appears in the first line of [*The
Awakening*]. Although Chopin refers to the bird as "he"—perhaps a deliberately ironic touch (Chopin knows from her first
sentence that the spirits of men and woman are really not so
different)—scholars seldom interpret "his" situation as anything but female. Wendy Martin, for example, sees him as a
symbol of domesticity, a wild bird "tamed for the amusement
of the household." As such a symbol, he becomes part of a
symbol pattern that had been historically very common in
women's literature.

⟨. . .⟩ Chopin's selection of the parrot to hint at Edna's
dilemma has significance beyond its representation of her
caged condition, however. First, unlike other caged birds
Chopin might have selected, the parrot (probably a yellow-
naped Amazon, though the makers of the film *Grand Isle* chose
a macaw) imitates what it hears. [Chopin critic Per] Seyersted
calls the parrot and the mockingbird "caged imitators, the one
repeating its master's words, the other echoing the voice of
other species." Symbolically, Chopin's parrot emphasizes the
force and prevalence of imitation in society. Chopin's parrot
speaks the language of the cosmopolitan New Orleans visitors
who reside at Grand Isle in the summers. He speaks Spanish
and French and English—but also, significantly, "a language
which nobody understood."

The parrot's language, then, is important symbolically not
only because it represents Edna's tendency to imitate, but
also because it hints at the need to discover and form new
linguistic (and behavioral) patterns once mimicked speech

has been discarded. Michael Gilmore describes the parrot as a "key symbol" in understanding Edna's desire for "authentic language." He observes that Edna becomes less and less inhibited, less and less a mimic of those around her, she begins "to utter sentiments unintelligible to her companions," sentiments, for example, about a willingness to sacrifice her life for her children—but not to sacrifice herself. Patricia Yeager, using Jacques Lacan and Michel Foucault, even suggests that the parrot "inhabits a multilingual culture and suggests the babble and lyricism bred by mixing world views."

Like the parrot, most of us live and speak by imitation, as do most of the characters in *The Awakening*. So how will we know how to speak, or what to say, when we have only ourselves to listen to? And should we somehow miraculously be able to find the words and language that are ours, will anyone be able to understand us? Will we ourselves be able to translate our words into meaningful patterns, patterns of both speech and action?

For a parrot, and for a human being, freedom is not an easy matter. Like the domesticated parrot in the novel, Edna is vulnerable when she is free. She has been cared for too long by an owner and taught a language not her own. Also like a parrot, Edna has had her wings clipped so often that she will spend all of her remaining days trying to recover the strength and imagination it takes to soar.

Here, and in her other writing, the unattractive or comic depiction of the parrot reinforces Chopin's belief that imitation in our lives is detestable. The parrot represents Edna before she awakens: had she remained like the parrot, Chopin would undoubtedly have seen her as pathetic rather than sympathetic. In an 1894 diary entry from her volume of "Impressions," Chopin describes her personal aversion to parrots; this entry also anticipates her future selection of the parrot as a symbol for dullness and stupidity: "I have no leaning toward a parrot. I think them detestable birds with their blinking stupid eyes and heavy clumsy motions. I never could become attached to one. . . . It made me positively ill today when I had gone to pass a few hours with Blanche [probably her cousin Blanche Bordley], to be forced to divide her society and attention with her own parrot and a neighbor's which she had borrowed. Fancy any sane human being doubling up an affliction in that way."

—Joyce Dyer, *"The Awakening": A Novel of Beginning* (New York: Twayne Publishers, 1993), pp. 34, 35–37

❖

Works by Kate Chopin

At Fault. 1890.

The Awakening. 1899.

Bayou Folk. 1894.

The Complete Works of Kate Chopin. Ed. Per Seyersted.
2 vols. 1969.

A Kate Chopin Miscellany. Ed. Per Seyersted and Emily Toth.
1979.

A Night in Acadie. 1897.

A Vocation and a Voice. Ed. Emily Toth. 1991.

Works About
Kate Chopin and
The Awakening

Allen, Priscilla. "Old Critics and New: The Treatment of Chopin's *The Awakening*" in *The Authority of Experience: Essays in Feminist Criticism*, ed. Aryln Diamond and Lee R. Edwards. Amherst: University of Massachusetts Press, 1977, 224–38.

Anonymous. *Dial* 27 (1 August 1899), 75.

Anonymous. *New York Times Saturday Review* (24 June 1899), 408.

Arner, Robert. "Kate Chopin," *Louisiana Studies* 14 (Spring 1975), 11–139.

Bloom, Harold, ed. *Kate Chopin*. Modern Critical Views Series. New York: Chelsea House, 1987.

Bonner, Thomas, Jr. "Kate Chopin's *At Fault* and *The Awakening*: A Study in Structure," *Markham Review* 7 (Fall 1977), 10–14.

Boren, Lynda S. and Sara deSaussure Davis, eds. *Kate Chopin Reconsidered: Beyond the Bayou*. Baton Rouge: Louisiana State University Press, 1992.

Cantwell, Robert. "*The Awakening* by Kate Chopin," Georgia Review 10 (Winter 1956), 489–94.

Casale, Ottavio Mark. "Beyond Sex: The Dark Romanticism of Kate Chopin's *The Awakening*," *Ball State University Forum* 19, no. 1 (Winter 1978), 76–80.

Christ, Carol P. *Diving Deep and Surfacing: Women Writers on Spiritual Quest*. Boston: Beacon Press, 1980.

Culley, Margaret, ed. *"The Awakening": An Authoritative Text, Contexts, Criticism.* New York: W. W. Norton, 1976.

Curtin, William, ed. *Willa Cather's Articles and Reviews.* Lincoln: University of Nebraska Press, 1970, Vol. 2, 697–99.

Donovan, Josephine. "Feminist Style Criticism," *Images of Women in Fiction: Feminist Perspectives*, ed. Susan Keppelman Cornillon. Bowling Green: Popular Press, 1972, 344–48.

Dyer, Joyce. "Lafcadio Hearn's *Chita* and Kate Chopin's *The Awakening*: Two Naturalistic Tales of the Gulf Islands," *Southern Studies* 23, no. 4 (Winter 1984), 412–26.

Fletcher, Marie. "The Southern Woman in the Fiction of Kate Chopin," *Southern Studies* 24, no. 1 (Spring 1966), 117–32.

Goldman, Dorothy. "Kate Chopin's *The Awakening*: 'Casting Aside that Fictitious Self'," *The Modern American Novella*, ed. A. Robert Lee. New York: St. Martin's Press, 1989, 48–65.

Jones, Anne Goodwyn. *Tomorrow Is Another Day: The Woman Writer in the South 1859–1936.* Baton Rouge: Louisiana State University Press, 1981.

Kearns, Katherine, "The Nullifications of Edna Pontellier," *American Literature* 63, no. 1 (March 1991), 62–88.

Koloski, Bernard. "Notes: The Swinburne Lines in *The Awakening*," *American Literature* 45 (January 1974), 608–10.

Lant, Kathleen Margaret. "The Siren of Grand Isle: Adele's Role in *The Awakening*," *Southern Studies* 23, no. 2 (Summer 1984), 167–75.

Lattin, Patricia Hopkins. "Childbirth and Motherhood in Kate Chopin's Fiction," *Regionalism and the Female Imagination* 4 (Spring 1978), 8–12.

Leary, Lewis. "Kate Chopin, Liberationist?," *Southern Literary Journal* 3 (Fall 1970), 138–44.

Leary, Lewis. *Southern Excursions: Essays on Mark Twain and Others*. Baton Rouge: Louisiana State University Press, 1971.

Leder, Priscilla. "An American Dilemma: Cultural Conflict in Kate Chopin's *The Awakening*," *Southern Studies* 22, no. 1 (1983), 97–104.

May, John R. "Local Color in *The Awakening*," *Southern Review* 6 (Autumn 1970), 1031–40.

Mitsutani, Margaret. "Kate Chopin's *The Awakening*: The Narcissism of Edna Pontellier, " *Studies in English Literature* (1986), 3–15.

Per Seyersted. *Kate Chopin: A Critical Autobiography*. Baton Rouge: Louisiana State University Press, 1969.

Ringe, Donald A. "Romantic Imagery in Kate Chopin's *The Awakening*," *American Literature* 43 (January 1972), 580–88.

Rosen, Kenneth. "Kate Chopin's *The Awakening*: Ambiguity as Art," *Journal of American Studies* 5 (August 1975), 197–99.

Spacks, Patricia Meyer. *The Female Imagination*. New York: Knopf, 1975.

Spangler, George. "Kate Chopin's *The Awakening*: A Partial Dissent," *Novel: A Forum on Fiction* 3 (Spring 1970), 249–55.

Stein, Allen F. "Kate Chopin," *After the Vows Were Spoken: Marriage in American Literary Realism*. Columbus: Ohio State University Press, 1984, 163–208.

Thornton, Lawrence. "*The Awakening*: A Political Romance," *American Literature* 52, no. 1 (March 1980), 50–66.

Toth, Emily. *Kate Chopin: A Life of the Author of "The Awakening."* New York: William Morrow, 1990.

Treichler, Paula A. "The Construction of Ambiguity in *The Awakening*: A Linguistic Analysis," *Women and Language in Literature and Society*, ed. Sally McConnell-Ginet, Ruth Borker, and Nelly Furman. New York: Praeger, 1980, 239–57.

Walker, Nancy. "Feminist or Naturalist: The Social Context of Kate Chopin's *The Awakening*," *Southern Quarterly* 17, no. 2 (1979), 95–103.

Wheeler, Otis B. "The Five Awakenings of Edna Pontellier," *Southern Review* 11 (January 1975), 118–28.

Wilson, Edmund. *Patriotic Gore: Studies in the Literature of the American Civil War.* New York: Oxford University Press, 1962.

Ziff, Larzer. *The American 1890s: Life and Times of a Lost Generation*. New York: Viking Press, 1966.

Index of
Themes and Ideas